Seeing Ourselves in Nature

Seeing Ourselves in Nature

Stories from Educators and Children of Indigenous, Black, and Other People of the Global Majority

Edited by Jessica Fong, MA, MEd

Redleaf Press®
www.redleafpress.org
800-423-8309

Published by Redleaf Press
10 Yorkton Court
St. Paul, MN 55117
www.redleafpress.org

First edition 2025
Cover design by Erin Kirk
Cover photograph by Adobe Stock/roman
Interior design by Louise OFarrell
Typeset in Adobe Minion
Printed in the United States of America
32 31 30 29 28 27 26 25 1 2 3 4 5 6 7 8

Library of Congress Cataloging-in-Publication Data
Names: Fong, Jessica (Educator), editor.
Title: Seeing ourselves in nature : stories from educators and children of indigenous, black, and other people of the global majority / edited by Jessica Fong, MA, MEd.
Description: First edition. | St. Paul, MN : Redleaf Press, [2025] | Includes bibliographical references and index. | Summary: "In Seeing Ourselves in Nature, author and editor Jessica Fong asks how Black and Brown educators in the United States create space for predominantly Black and Brown children and families to reconnect to nature"—Provided by publisher.
Identifiers: LCCN 2025007334 (print) | LCCN 2025007335 (ebook) | ISBN 9781605548296 (paperback ; alk. paper) | ISBN 9781605548302 (ebook)
Subjects: LCSH: Place-based education—United States. | Nature study—United States. | Outdoor education—United States. | Minority teachers—United States. | Children of minorities—Education—United States. | School children—United States—Social conditions. | Discrimination in education—United States.
Classification: LCC LC239 .S44 2025 (print) | LCC LC239 (ebook) | DDC 370.11/5—dc23/eng/20250501
LC record available at https://lccn.loc.gov/2025007334
LC ebook record available at https://lccn.loc.gov/2025007335

Printed on acid-free paper

To the little girl devouring books at 1:00 a.m., you couldn't have imagined this moment and, yes, you are still a night owl.

A mis papás, convivo con las hormigas y acarició las flores por la influencia de ustedes y por eso, gracias. Los amo.

A mi chulo, Matías, words cannot express how you have changed my life. Your tiny feet stomping in the equally tiny streams at the conservatory inspired me to see things anew. Nature *could* be anywhere, in those small streams and in our urban backyard. *Te amo*.

Contents

Acknowledgments

I am deeply grateful to everyone who has supported me throughout the writing and publication of this book.

To my editor, Melissa York, for her insightful guidance and unwavering support.

To Ellen Doris and David Sobel, who not only believed in my vision but also used their influence and connections to help make this dream a reality. You are the allies we need on the road to equity.

To my family and friends, for their constant love and support.

To every single author in this book, I am profoundly honored to have walked alongside you and now stand with you as your stories are brought into the world. Your voices are what we all need in this moment. I am overjoyed that your time has come.

And to everyone at Redleaf, for their hard work and dedication in bringing this book to life. You listened and responded to my vision, and this book is a testament to that.

¡Muchísimas gracias!

INTRODUCTION

Heartsick Joy and the Paradox of Language

Jessica Fong, Chicago, IL

As I put pen to proverbial paper to write an introduction to this captivating collection of stories, I find myself reflecting on my own connection to nature as a Latine person. Immediately my thoughts go to the language that inhabits my tongue. The Spanish language is by nature a love letter to nature. It is uniquely suited to describe the inherent duality in the natural world. It is a language that exists in both the eternal and the ephemeral, since it has two verbs to describe the act of being: the verbs *ser* and *estar*. Both verbs mean "to be," but *ser* indicates a permanent state, while *estar* refers to a state of being that is impermanent or transient. You can be a happy person, as part of your personality: *Soy una persona feliz*, or you can be happy just right now, at this moment: *Estoy feliz*. With *ser* and *estar*, Spanish provides us with a way to encounter and describe nature as an eternal and everlasting cycle of life, as well as capture its beautiful impermanence. The American robin can be beautiful as an element of nature, and it can be beautiful just now, in this moment, prancing across the damp spring-green grass, showing off its rusty-red breast. This duality typifies the *colibrí*, the hummingbird, a bird significant to the ancient Aztec and modern Mexican culture for this quality. This small, fragile creature with seemingly limitless energy performs feats of agility and endurance while maintaining an incredibly efficient yet fleeting existence.

This same duality lives within the Spanish language. Spanish infuses speakers with a paradox that sits on our tongues and melds into our hearts and minds while feeling foreign to our ancestral spirit. It makes perfect sense that Spanish has taught me about the paradoxes of nature. The very language I speak leads to paradoxical situations, contradictions, and intriguing nuances that, like *ser* and *estar*, are part of who I am.

Yet I must immediately acknowledge Spanish as the language of the colonizing oppressor, forced into the mouths of the native people of Latin America while simultaneously erasing their mother tongue. The legacy of colonization has left a complicated relationship that we, Black and Brown folks, dance with our entire lives. We feel the push and pull of growing up in a world where many things—from our culture to our language—originate in the brutal history of colonization, while wanting desperately to return to our Indigenous roots and reconnect to the land.

This lost connection was a tool of the colonizer, wielded with intention and causing lasting damage. If the native people of the land lost their language, they couldn't communicate with one another to organize and rise up. The same was true for the enslaved African people forced to come to the Americas. Without the ability to communicate with one another, we couldn't maintain our connection to the land, and we couldn't be self-sufficient and empowered. Yet, people of color are resilient. Our connection to the land, while reduced, was not completely lost, due to the work of our elders. For many Black and Brown people, this dance between the culture we developed because of our resilience and the culture we lost because of the trauma creates a sense of being *de aquí, de allá, y de nuestros antepasados* (from here, from over there, and from our ancestors). It's a sense of *anhelo*, yearning, that brings its own sadness and joy. This same paradox drives us to deep insight and exploration into our very own existence and identity. It drives a feeling of heartsickness in me. Whenever I hear the language of Indigenous peoples in the Americas spoken and sung, I cry. Tears slide down my face as I am overwhelmed with the beauty of the languages and the weariness of the loss of those languages and culture for my family, myself, and my son.

Even with all these complexities, I acknowledge that Spanish is the language that connects me to nature. As a Romance language, Spanish uses gendered nouns with articles like *el* and *la*—another way to relate to nature that doesn't exist in English. A black and white stray cat in the neighborhood is not just a cat, a nondescript animal, but rather it's *el gato* or *la gata*. The articles *el* and *la* transform the animal from a neutral object—a simple "it"—to a being with gender, immediately bringing me closer to the cat as I imagine it as a boy cat or a girl cat. Living beings have characteristics that make them male or female, and although our ideas of gender are in flux, our awareness or attribution of gender to living things shapes the way we interact with the natural world. *El árbol*, the tree, becomes masculine. *La flor*, the flower, becomes feminine. *El pájaro*, the bird, becomes masculine. *La naturaleza*, nature, is feminine.

Each article breathes life into the noun, assigning it qualities that we associate with that gender. "Feminine" nouns may be soft, kind, benevolent, and fecund, while "masculine" nouns might be imbued with the stereotypically male attributes of strength, stoicism, sturdiness, and virility. It's a complicated relationship, as scientists have found that nature is not binary, and many Indigenous languages do not use gendered nouns and articles. Yet, throughout my life, the gendered articles and nouns of my language have colored my connection with the natural beings they describe, making my connection to nature stronger and more personal.

Natural beings have played an integral part in the story of my life. "*Las plantitas son agradecidas.*" Here again that paradox of *ser* and *estar* comes as my *mami* tells me about plants being *agradecidas*, grateful, as part of their very being with the use of the conjugation *son* of the verb *ser*. The *plantitas* are grateful now and will always be grateful. In Guatemala and in Chicago, plants were a rich part of my childhood as I helped my *mami* care for her indoor and outdoor plants. Thinking about flowers being grateful takes me back to a scene in the 1951 *Alice in Wonderland* movie from Walt Disney, when Alice lands in a patch of flowers. The flowers *cobran vida*, come to life and sing and dance with Alice looking on. Anytime my *mami* refers to flowers and plants being *agradecidas,* I imagine I'm Alice dancing along with the flowers. In that moment, I'm a child lying in a field of flowers chatting and dancing around me. They are my *plantita* friends. The plants appreciate the love and care I give them because we are in communion with one another. My *aliento*, my breath and my life force, dances with theirs and becomes part of a circular interaction that brings life to us all. Perhaps, as a child who spent a lot of time alone, I needed the flowers and plants to become part of my world—to keep me company.

My mami was not my only teacher in developing my relationship with nature. My *papi* also played a supporting role. In my childhood, my *papi* threw my sister and I into nature, literally. An ex-military man from Guatemala, his motto was, and continues to be, to take challenges head on. If my *papi* were an animal, he would be the otter parent who grabs pups by the scruff and drags them into the water. While my *mami* would be a wood duck, gently quacking to coax her chicks into the water.

I have a vivid core memory of cicadas from when I was about seven or eight years old. It was a hot, sunny summer day, maybe early June. My family would often go on nature walks in one of the forest preserves surrounding the city of Chicago, and this was just one of those regular walk days. I remember large bushes along the path, the small green leaves and thin branches brushing my arms as I walked by. Farther along, I began to hear a strange hum. For anyone who has never heard a brood of cicadas, the sound is hard to describe. It's deafening and rhythmic—the sound you would imagine the universe makes in its deep, dark depths but with a tinge of annoyance.

I heard them and then I saw them. The bushes vibrated with the bodies of the cicadas as one huge buzzing mass. Confronting them in such a massive quantity for the first time, I was justifiably terrified. I froze in horror. My *papi*, being the person he is, told me "*No tengas miedo,*" "Don't be afraid," and pushed me forward, straight into the bush full of the humming, clicking, whining cicadas. It was the loving type of push bird parents do every spring, but a push, nonetheless. Sheer terror turned to surprise when I wasn't eaten alive. I took a giant step out of the bush, shaken. I'd never been terrified of an insect before, so why was I now? Perhaps it was the vast amount of them. I shuffled my feet closer to the bush I had just been inside of and realized the cicadas were fascinating. They were large and unsettling and beautiful with their transparent, black-veined wings and bulging reddish-orange eyes. I reached to pick one off the bush, and it held on to the spindly branch with all the might its teeny legs could muster. The branch bent wildly and finally gave way, boomeranging away from me and back, as I held the hard-shelled little insect between my thumb and forefinger. The fear dissolved and was replaced by curiosity.

My hope for this book is to illuminate the vibrant stories of children, families, and educators of color as they develop deep, joyful connections to nature. I hope to be like J. Drew Lanham, one of many Black authors who has brought to the forefront the way Black and Brown people connect to nature. His personal, historical, and cultural narratives of nature bring a much-needed representation. He says, "Joy is the justice we give ourselves. Nature brings me joy. And that to me is justice" (Lanham 2024). Reclaiming joy in nature is an act of resistance and movement toward justice for people of color. Nature brings the human spirit joy, and nowhere is that truer than with young children. Lanham goes on to say, "If life is heard in our neighborhoods, it brings us joy when the robin warbles in concert with the laughter of children." In this book, educators of color pass on their knowledge of the many ways they find joy with nature. They share their insights on what they have done to create these experiences of joy for the children and families they serve. Their hope is that you will be inspired to do the same in your own context.

Years later, faced with the daunting task of putting pen to paper for a college admissions essay, I remembered the cicadas. And so it was that millions of cicadas got me into Northwestern University. Perhaps it was thousands, but it felt like millions. And again, many years after college, as a mother, I found myself filled with rueful nostalgia when my two-year-old son mimicked the cicada's sound. "Reeurr, reeeuurrr, reeeuurrrrrrrr," he said with a giggle on a hot June day—the same curiosity I had as a child but matched with a joyful experience.

Why This Book at This Moment

These experiences and many more that are special to my Guatemalan family and culture have brought me to this moment. I am blessed to be uplifting the stories of other people of color who also had these unique experiences in nature by way of their culture. These stories have been untold in the mainstream narrative for generations even as countless White, nature-based researchers have been given the space to tell the stories of White children and families. Our stories stay alive with each and every breath taken by Black and Brown people. These stories, having existed for generations, teach us about being part of something larger than ourselves. The lack of these stories creates a lack of agency for people of color in nature. Where we don't see ourselves, we feel we don't belong. Yet we connect to nature in everyday moments, tending plants in a small balcony garden and in the cicada-filled woods.

The paucity of the stories of Black and Brown folks in nature creates a hole as wide as that left by a giant sequoia felled in the redwood forests of the West Coast. The void left behind is immense in both physical space and ecological impact. And these experiences are as timeless and as vital to the story of the human connection to nature as those trees are irreplaceable and ancient in their ecosystem.

The stories of people of color in nature have been appropriated and, worse, intentionally ignored, to the detriment of our people and planet. Our stories created the landscape, both figuratively and literally. Black cowboys made up almost a third of the cowboys in the United States, by some estimates. Yet these cowboys are not known or celebrated the way the White cowboys are. Surfing is believed to have originated five thousand years ago with the ancient

Indigenous people of Peru, who used *caballitos de totora*—small watercrafts made from totora grass—for fishing and recreation. By AD 400, *he'e nalu* (surfing) had emerged among Indigenous Polynesians, where it held deep spiritual significance. Though it was suppressed by White colonizers in the 1800s, Native Hawaiians preserved it as a cultural refuge during colonization and unrest, even using it as a form of resistance against segregationist policies.

Even when the stories of Black and Brown people become part of the White, Eurocentric narrative, the stories are not told with their full and complete truth. But if told with fidelity, these stories would show just how powerful and knowledgeable Black and Brown people are. The full story of Harriet Tubman is just one example of a history that has been suppressed. The established tale of Harriet Tubman focuses on how she led people to freedom on the Underground Railroad. That part of her work has been lauded, and rightfully so. Yet, she was also a naturalist who used her profound knowledge of the natural world on her many journeys between North and South.

Harriet was born to enslaved parents and worked as a field hand, among other duties, learning the skills she needed to safely lead the way to freedom. Harriet used her knowledge of the land and the skies to slip unseen through the night. It's hard for modern people to imagine just how pitch-black the night can truly be outside of the range of electric lights. On nights devoid of the moon, it can be impossible to see your hand in front of your face, and yet Harriet led approximately seventy people through dense forest and swamps using her expertise. Angela Crenshaw, a ranger at the Harriet Tubman Underground Railroad State Park, calls her "the ultimate outdoors woman," who used an owl call to let people know when it was safe to continue their dangerous trek (Keyes 2020). Harriet also had a deep understanding of the plants that could serve as food and medicine and knew how to trap animals to eat. Her depth of knowledge and skills is almost unimaginable to a modern city dweller. I can only imagine that Harriet relied on her learned skills as well as the skills in her blood. As Shelton Johnson writes, "We are all descended from Native people, from African people, and those blood memories are barely beneath the surface of our people." He goes on to say, "The African within all of us is just waiting for the opportunity to walk, discover, and explore again. Give her or him that moment of spirit, of grace, to awaken our bodies, minds, and souls to the joy of being Indigenous again, children again, exploring wild new worlds" (Mapp 2022, 9).

At this moment in our planet's history, we are realizing what happens when we ignore the relationship we have with the land. Indigenous peoples lived in balance with nature since time immemorial, using planting techniques that included intentional burning, crop rotation, and companion planting. Tribes such as the Choctaw use these techniques to this day. Other tribes that lived a more nomadic lifestyle lived in harmony with nature by honoring the spirits of the animals they relied on and using every part. The Lakota tribe relied heavily on the buffalo and used every part for food, clothing, and shelter. The Lakota followed a seasonal migration pattern and moved to different areas based on the availability of resources, preventing overuse of the land. And yet, all Indigenous peoples in North America, whether nomadic or sedentary, were systematically and forcefully removed from their lands. We are now witnessing the consequences of breaking the deep connection between the land and its people. I often wonder with *anhelo* what the natural world would look like if all Indigenous people had stayed on their land. What would the world look like if colonization had never happened? Would we all still have that understanding in our bones that plants are *agradecidas* and cicadas can teach? Would climate change be a reality?

This book is a heartfelt effort to amplify the voices of Black and Brown educators in the United States who are working to give children that "moment of spirit" to reconnect to our Indigenous and ancestral blood. Just as time is given to understanding how trauma lives in our bodies, the same amount of time, or more, should be given to connecting to the power that lives in our bodies with the knowledge of our ancestors who lived in communion with the land with each footfall. As Rue Mapp (2022) writes in her book *Nature Swagger*, "Connecting people to nature is actually a journey inward and a homecoming with oneself" (22). Mapp's book inspired me to reconnect with my own relationship to nature and sparked the idea for a book that would center the stories of Black and Brown nature educators. The guiding question for this book is: In what ways do Black and Brown educators in the United States create space for predominantly Black and Brown children and families to build a relationship with nature? This book is a small step toward bringing these understandings front and center, where they should have always been. Our stories demand to be told.

It is essential to recognize that this book emerges from the context of historical and systemic racism in the United States. Some of the authors discuss topics related to this context. I urge readers who are not familiar with this complex history to do their own research and work to understand why the stories in this book are so important.

Resources for additional learning about systemic and historical racism in the United States:

Hannah-Jones, Nikole. 2021. *The 1619 Project: A New Origin Story.* One World.

Kendi, Ibram X. 2016. *Stamped from the Beginning.* Avalon Publishing Group.

———. 2019. *How to Be an Antiracist.* Bodley Head.

Kimmerer, Robin Wall. 2015. *Braiding Sweetgrass: Indigenous Wisdom, Scientific Knowledge, and the Teachings of Plants.* Milkweed Press.

Love, Bettina. 2020. *We Want to Do More Than Survive: Abolitionist Teaching and the Pursuit of Educational Freedom.* Beacon Press.

Oluo, Ijeoma. 2019. *So You Want to Talk About Race.* Seal Press.

Wilkerson, Isabel. 2023. *Caste: The Origins of Our Discontents.* Random House.

The Big Benefits of Nature-Based Play and Learning

The justice of nature extends beyond joy to equitable access to nature connection. A broad and growing body of research shows that nature-based play and learning provides countless benefits for young learners. The report "Nature Preschools in the United States: 2022 Survey" from the Natural Start Alliance observes that regardless of what type of outdoor experience children have, or where they have these experiences, the positive impact can be felt in the following areas:

- enhancing brain development
- improving academic performance
- enhancing communication
- promoting social-emotional development
- promoting emotional resilience and self-regulation
- promoting executive functioning
- providing mental health benefits
- reducing symptoms of ADHD
- providing therapeutic benefits to children with autism
- promoting physical activity and motor development (Natural Start Alliance 2022)

Analysis of large data sets conducted in hundreds of peer-reviewed studies have confirmed these benefits so many times over that one group of researchers wrote, "It is time to take nature seriously as a resource for learning—particularly for students not effectively reached by traditional instruction" (Kuo, Barnes, and Jordan 2019). The benefits of nature-based learning and instruction also extend to the educators in these programs.

Still, we must acknowledge the backdrop of systemic racism, which has led to disparity in access to nature-based play and learning for children and families of color. The low number of children of color enrolled in preschool programs that use nature as an integral part of the curriculum is startling. The 2022 survey from the North American Association for Environmental Education (NAEE) reports the following statistics about nature-based preschools in the United States:

- The estimated number of nature-based preschools grew over 200 percent from 2017 to 2022, reaching around 800 programs. Despite this growth, the number of children of color enrolled in these programs saw no change.

- In 2017 ten thousand children were served annually in some form of nature preschool. By 2022 this number jumped to an estimated twenty-five thousand.
- In 2022 78 percent of children in these programs were White, even though they make up only 47.3 percent of the children in the United States overall. This means that White children are overrepresented in nature preschool programs, with Black and Brown children making up less than 15 percent.
- The racial makeup of staff in nature preschools mirrors that of the students:

  —15.8 percent of educators identify as Latinx, Black, Asian, or American Indian.

  —80.4 percent of educators are White.

- While White educators are also overrepresented in preschool and kindergarten programs nationally, the percentage of educators of color is slightly better than in nature programs:

  —16.7 percent Black

  —13.5 percent Latinx

  —4.2 percent Asian

Many educators of color who work in nature-based programs express a sense of being alone in this work. When I've presented my work at local and national conferences, I am one of a few people of color in the room. Often, I'll catch the eye of one of the few others and we will both smile, making a connection by acknowledging each other and lessening the sense of solitude. Many organizations, the Natural Start Alliance included, are working hard to uplift the stories and expertise of nature-based educators of color on their platforms, but so much more work is needed. Every Black and Brown child in the United States must have access to the benefits of nature-based learning. The current lack of it is a clear-cut example of environmental racism. We cannot stand on the sidelines while Black and Brown children continue to lose their connection to nature in the name of academic rigor and "catching up."

Nature-based learning has the potential to finally bring equity to the educational experiences of Black and Brown children, removing the systemic barriers that plague students of color in traditional educational settings and bringing justice-based education. By virtue of the work and the setting, this educational model focuses on curiosity, inquiry, and child-led learning. At its core, nature-based play and learning provide children with individualized experiences that take the whole child into account. As Iheoma Iruka and colleagues (2020) write, "It is critical to provide different learning modalities and opportunities for children to better meet their needs" (17).

It is clear that traditional, Eurocentric ways of teaching and learning are failing students of color. A report from the Department of Education (2021) titled "Discipline Practices in Preschool" found that 43.3 percent of black students in public schools received one or more suspensions, a rate that is 2.5 times greater than their share of the total preschool population. Remember, these are preschool children, only four to five years old, who are being suspended. These disheartening statistics point to grave injustice and a continuation of the systematic racism that Black and Brown children have faced from the dawn of the modern educational system. We are maintaining an inherently inequitable system. Nature is the answer, as it so often is.

What to Expect from This Book

This book is shared in four sections. We begin with authors who are working toward liberation and justice by actively pushing back against the pushing down of academics on children of color because they are "behind." We ask, who sets the standard for what "behind" looks like? These authors are creating spaces in their communities for joyful reconnection to nature for children and families to provide holistic and care-centered learning.

In section 2, community and cultural connections based in nature come to the forefront. These authors share the importance of seeing Brown faces in natural spaces, both in real life and in the images found in books. We agree with author and professor Michelle H. Martin (2019) as she writes, "Of course we know that race and socioeconomic status can matter a great deal when addressing the question of what conditions need to be favorable for children and families to spend more time outdoors; and given the limited portrayal of minoritized children having immersive experiences outdoors in children's picture books, this genre has fallen into the same trap." As a Girl Scout, Martin developed a deep love for the outdoors and advocates for children of color to have "immersive experiences outdoors." Martin shares the writing of J. Drew Lanham here to make a poignant point about being Black in the outdoors. Lanham writes in his 2016 book *The Home Place: Memoirs of a Colored Man's Love Affair with Nature*, "To be wild is to be colorful, and in the claims of colorfulness there's an embracing and a self-acceptance. . . . Wildness means living in the unknown." While Martin acknowledges that there are books that show children of color "enjoying the outdoors," these books do not often portray children and families of color being immersed in nature, connecting with it in a deeper level, and seeing themselves mirrored in the wild parts of the natural world.

In section 3, we encounter stories of four Black women who have made being in nature a radical act simply by sharing their joy. Through poetry and verse, these stories provide a new narrative for children of color in nature.

The final section of the book looks at how children harness their powerful curiosity and intrinsic motivation when interacting with nature. The stories in this section show how children and youth can delve deep into their learning through long projects when the focal point is the natural world. Often we educators assume young children have short attention spans and cannot focus or engage with concepts or ideas for long periods of time. The stories in this section provide a moving counterargument to these false narratives.

References

Department of Education. 2021. *Discipline Practices in Preschool.* DOE. https://civilrightsdata.ed.gov/assets/downloads/crdc-DOE-Discipline-Practices-in-Preschool-part1.pdf.

Iruka, Iheoma, Stephanie Curenton, and Tonia Durden. 2020. *Don't Look Away: Embracing Anti-Bias Classrooms.* Gryphon House.

Keyes, Allison. 2020. "Harriet Tubman, an Unsung Naturalist, Used Owl Calls as a Signal on the Underground Railroad." *Audubon*, February 25, 2020. www.audubon.org/news/harriet-tubman-unsung-naturalist-used-owl-calls-signal-underground-railroad.

Kuo, Ming, Michael Barnes, and Catherine Jordan. 2019. "Do Experiences with Nature Promote Learning? Converging Evidence of a Cause-and-Effect Relationship." *Frontiers in Psychology* 10. https://doi.org/10.3389/fpsyg.

Lanham, J. Drew. 2016. *The Home Place: Memoirs of a Colored Man's Love Affair with Nature.* Milkweed.

———. 2024. *2024 Openlands Annual Luncheon—Full Program.* YouTube, October 18. https://youtu.be/_irYObqsk9o?si=MROQCjiTAUptW8tO.

Mapp, Rue. 2022. *Nature Swagger: Stories and Vision of Black Joy in the Outdoors.* Chronicle.

Martin, Michelle H. 2019. "Black Kids Camp, Too . . . Don't They? Embracing 'Wildness' in Picture Books." *The Horn Book*, September 11, 2019. www.hbook.com/story/black-kids-camp-too.

Natural Start Alliance. 2022. *Nature Preschools in the United States: 2022 National Survey.* NAEE.

SECTION I

Pushing Back Against the Push Down

In November 2023, orcas took back their water. In an incident scientists are still unable to explain, a pod of orcas attacked and ultimately sank a yacht in the Straits of Gibraltar, a narrow passage of water between Spain and Morocco. This followed a string of similar incidents going back to 2020. No one knows why the orcas began to exhibit this aggressive behavior, and although some scientists theorize that the orcas are simply playing with the boats, I have a sense that perhaps the orcas realized it was calmer during the worldwide slowdown caused by COVID and wanted to take back their peace. There's no way to know, but perhaps the orcas were pushing back against a system that had been wreaking havoc on the natural world and prevented them from thriving.

To me, this idea—wishful thinking or not—of sentient beings understanding the detrimental effects a foreign system has had on their lives is analogous to the way we as educators and caregivers of color understand how the White, Eurocentric educational system has affected our children. We see the system overtly in the systemic racism we encounter every day, while we also feel it internally down to our very DNA. This understanding has led many nature-based educators of color to find progressive and "radical" ways of providing learning experiences for their students and for their own children. Often these ways are a return to what our ancestors did to relate to nature. The authors in this section have a depth of understanding of the detrimental effects the loss of nature has had on their families, their students, and their communities. Much like the orcas, these authors are pushing back and sinking metaphorical ships.

In this section, you will learn how Ashley Brailsford has unearthed joy for herself, her family, and her community and how she works to connect nature to the cultural understandings of people of color. Kameeka Shirley shares how she goes outside for liberation and uses nature to resist the social structures that hold BIPOC people down. Lotus Chaney recounts how she began her journey in Costa Rica to break the bonds of generational trauma and medical racism and returned to the United States with new understandings. By using documentation to make learning visible, Ron Grady asks us to consider how we engage with families of color and work to break the bonds of the false narrative of our children being "behind" when measured by inherently racist metrics. And finally, Vanessa Miot explores how nature provided her with a "cheat code" for raising her children to nurture their curiosity and center their experiences as Black children in nature.

Reflection Questions

1. How can you leverage the insights from the experiences of the authors to communicate the benefits of nature-based experiences to the families you work with?
2. How can you adapt and integrate ways to connect children with nature into your curriculum and empower families to continue these experiences outside the school day?
3. How can you foster a shared understanding and commitment to incorporating nature in families' routines and activities?

CHAPTER 1

Honoring Culture, Exploring Justice, and Unearthing Joy

Ashley Brailsford, Nashville, TN

Ashley Brailsford, PhD, is an early childhood educator and nature enthusiast. She launched the organization Unearthing Joy to guide the development of culturally centered, nature-based programming for families, community groups, and organizations that center the stories and contributions of Indigenous, Black, and other people of the global majority. Her experiences in teaching, professorship, curriculum development, and education leadership coupled with time spent as an outdoor guide inform her programming and development process to transform outdoor spaces into cultural spaces that honor culture, explore justice, and unearth joy.

When schools shut down in 2020 because of the COVID-19 pandemic and I was "liberated" from my day job, I found this the perfect opportunity to spend more time outside. I did not know in what direction my career would go, but I was certain that it would need to center joy. My son was five years old at the time, and I had already seen how his short time in a public kindergarten that limited outdoor activity was also shrinking his curiosity and sense of wonder. After all, he had previously attended a Montessori program for toddlers as well as two wonderful preschool programs that had greatly valued hours of outdoor play. To see him go from that environment into the public school setting, where the kids were lucky to get just fifteen minutes outside a day, was soul crushing.

As the fall of 2020 set in, I decided to homeschool my son and nurture his learning through the outdoors. But I knew he still needed community. Who am I fooling? *I* also needed community, because I knew homeschooling would be very different from my own public school teaching experiences. As I searched for outdoor programs in Nashville, I found that, unsurprisingly, many of these spaces were very White. So, I began to ask, what does a nature program look like that centers the experiences and roles of Indigenous, Black, and other people of the global majority? What does it look like when a program utilizes the framework of multicultural education that I had once taught back in graduate school? I needed to go back to my own childhood and outdoor experiences to find answers. I grew up spending a lot of time outdoors in Greensboro, North Carolina, in the late 1980s and 1990s. Aside from playing outside all day every

Author as a child

day in our neighborhood, I was part of an all-Black Girl Scout troop that went on camping trips and other outdoor adventures. I spent summers and some weekends at my grandparents' farms in rural North Carolina and South Carolina shucking corn, plucking plums, and "swimming" in a giant washtub to stay cool.

Why do I share these familial stories? We may tend to think of a culture or nature expert as someone with a title or specialized degree, but in reality, expertise can be developed within our own families and in our own communities. There is rich knowledge all around us, and we must be open to looking for it in unconventional ways.

I also want folks to understand that teaching about, in, and through nature deserves to happen in the context of the cultures who have stewarded this planet from the beginning of time. When I was living in Charleston, South Carolina, and teaching at the College of Charleston, I joined an outdoor group to explore the area. This group aimed to engage Black people in nature exploration, and often the volunteer leader would tie our excursions to local African American history. This experience opened my eyes to the understanding that Black folks have always been in relationship with nature, whether through recreation, for lifestyle, or for respite. I knew these stories were important to tell as I began Unearthing Joy, the organization I founded to create culturally centered nature programs.

When I first started offering programming for families and children through Unearthing Joy, I wanted to find a permanent space in a historically significant Black neighborhood to show that our spaces were thriving with nature too. I began volunteering at Brooklyn Heights Community Garden in Nashville, Tennessee, in June 2020 so I could be safe outside of my home during the pandemic while also fulfilling this immense internal desire to reconnect with the land. I intentionally chose a space that was stewarded by a Black woman as I shifted into thinking more intentionally about how I was supporting Black and Indigenous land stewardship efforts. I was asking questions around who owns land and how we utilize land to support healing and well-being.

I got to know Ms. Pearl, the founder of the community garden, as we planted, weeded, and harvested together weekly. I asked her if I could host immersive experiences in the garden. Soon after, we learned some fascinating information about the history of the neighborhood. An artist, Arthur Haynes, once lived on the street. He wrote in a book that his father did not value play for children, so Arthur wanted there to be spaces for children to play in the neighborhood. Additionally, we learned about residents who had fought a zoning plan for new development in 1985 because they desired more green space for the children to play. At that same time, neighborhood residents organized a food co-op to improve access to fresh food in the neighborhood.

We learned this history as we were redeveloping the mission of Brooklyn Heights Community Garden to reflect a focus on growing food, intergenerational learning, and creative play as our pillars. The parallels we felt between the garden's mission and the neighborhood's history are profound. But more than anything, for me, learning these stories revealed the importance of knowing and understanding the lands we inhabit and steward, as the land often holds the solutions for the challenges our communities may be facing.

This legacy of the land where Brooklyn Heights Community Garden is located demonstrates why the strategies I use to create culturally centered programs and share with other educators must be grounded in the narratives and experiences of Indigenous, Black, and other people of the global majority. These strategies include the following:

1. Examining biases through an antiracist lens
2. Shifting our mindsets about what counts as nature
3. Building relationships with community members
4. Creating an inclusive environment
5. Transforming programs and curriculum to center our stories and roles
6. Advocating for equitable structures and justice
7. Inspiring joy

My son with Ms. Pearl

Transforming programs and curriculum to center our stories can include tools such as multicultural literature, art, music, technology, and interviews. One of the learning opportunities I created with my son was interviewing Ms. Pearl. I asked him if we were to interview her about Brooklyn Heights and gardening, what questions would he ask? We sat down together to brainstorm a list of questions. At the time, my son was not interested in writing at all, so rather

Ms. Pearl drumming

than forcing him to write, I wrote down the questions as he brainstormed. I gave him my phone and said he could record his interview with Ms. Pearl. It was powerful to witness a six-year-old taking charge of the interview process, showing the confidence to ask his questions and to hear the responses. We placed the interview clips into a slideshow with the questions presented on each slide. Interviews are a great way to unearth stories in our communities. Good interview subjects can include children's family members or community members who have knowledge and skills connected to nature.

My desire to provide opportunities for children to interview and spend time with community members who have knowledge and skills became the basis of the programs I designed for Unearthing Joy. Our sessions last an hour. I start them with an opening circle to welcome everyone and read a multicultural book related to our topic for the day; then we have an activity for forty minutes. We end with a closing circle for the children and families to share what brought them joy that day.

The first six-week series I offered was called Gardening for Food Justice. As I was still new to gardening, I invited Ms. Pearl to cofacilitate some of the sessions. She offered a spiritual and cultural element to our series, explaining why it is important to honor the land before we plant. During one session, she demonstrated this through dance and drumming. We planted foods the children liked to eat, talked about the experience of food apartheid (see sidebar) in the neighborhood, and considered how we could share our food to support food justice efforts.

Food apartheid **is the intentional and systemic exclusion of historically excluded communities from access to fresh and nutritious food. The term, introduced by food activist Karen Washington, has replaced** ***food desert*** **to acknowledge the conscious harm those in power perpetuate around the food systems of communities of color. Unlike a desert, which is a natural earth phenomenon, apartheid is a human construct, and the use of the term brings to the forefront the system of legalized, unequal separation of people of color from nutritious food.**

For the fall, I wanted to do something about "wilderness skills," but I had to challenge the surface definition of this term, as for me it conjured images of people who love to be outdoors and who do not mind having minimal amenities. But when I thought about wilderness skills—building fires, foraging, making medicine from plants, cooking, navigating, and so on—I realized these were all skills our ancestors possessed. These skills were not "nice to know," but indeed necessary for their way of life, and I also realized they were key skills for our liberation from oppressive systems. So I called the series Skills for Liberation, and I invited parents with these skill sets to lead the sessions.

For the next series, Creative Arts in Nature, I explored unconventional ways of engaging families and children in nature and the outdoors by incorporating different artistic media. I invited various creatives, including a musician and a photographer, to lead sessions presenting their art and its connection to nature. A friend organization, Recycle Reinvest, held a class in making tote bags from old T-shirts. A parent led a flower printmaking session.

The last series I created was about animals, at the request of the parents and children. Several sessions were led by a zookeeper. We also hosted a beekeeper, a poultry farmer, and a representative from a local river advocacy group who taught us about aquatic species and ways to protect them.

My son with vegetables

Victoria with sopas

Tolani with bee frame

In putting together these programs, it was crucially important to me that our Black and Brown children would see themselves in these roles, so the speakers had to reflect a diverse group of backgrounds. I was very intentional about asking community members and nature organizations to recommend Black and Brown people who had knowledge and skills to share with our groups. I always offered compensation for their time, as too often Black and Brown people are asked to provide their knowledge for free. All of these values and strategies shape how we do programming, and I continue to learn and gain new ideas.

One of the key things for programs to keep in mind is that the strategies and ideas we use can be adapted, and these are only a few of many, many possible strategies. There are many programs doing culturally centered work, and I am excited to be part of a collective of educators who are sharing the ways they center nature play in early childhood.

Reflection Questions

1. Think about the community or location(s) where you work with children and families. What are the stories of that land and of that community, both past and present, that might be overlooked?

2. Think about the street names or the names of buildings. Who are they named after? Why are these people significant? Whose stories are untold that should be told? What did we learn from those stories that informs how we use the land or how we honor it?

3. What are the skills and talents of the children, parenting adults, neighbors, and family members in your community that could be shared in relationship to nature and your children's interest?

4. How might you use interviews, multicultural literature, the creative arts, or technology to transform your curriculum?

CHAPTER 2

Outdoors for Social Justice

Kameeka Shirley, Dade City, FL

Kameeka Shirley holds a bachelor's degree in business administration and marketing and worked in finance in New York before joining Teach for America as a 2017 corps member in Jacksonville, Florida. Most recently, she has worked as a Montessori classroom teacher and holds a Florida teaching license with a reading endorsement. She has completed coursework in English as a Second Language and Gifted education and earned an Early Childhood Montessori credential. Outside of her time in the classroom, Kameeka is a mother and serves on the National Advisory Board of The Collective, Teach for America's Association for BIPOC Alumni.

Outdoors for social justice. Outdoors for liberation. Outdoors for connection.

It's easier to step outside than it is to change social structures. Let's face it: We are raising young humans in a society that is grounded in the values of "grind culture"—competition, materialism, and self-determination—which have bred societal ills, including social- and self-disconnection, racism, poverty, and inequality. These ills are more than metaphorical. Confronting the ongoing trauma and stress of racism, sexism, inequality, and poverty manifests itself within our bodies, resulting in, as authors Gabor and Daniel Maté put it, "a familiar brew of disturbed genetic function, inflammation, chromosomal and cellular aging, physiological wear and tear, hormonal disturbances, cardiovascular effects and immune debility" (2022, chapter 22). Black mothers die giving birth at almost three times the rate of non-Hispanic White mothers. Their infants are at least twice as likely to die as White babies (Ely and Driscoll 2023). This startling statistic holds true across education levels and socioeconomic status. And as those babies grow into young children and face further stress from the traumas of racism and/or poverty, it affects the areas associated with memory and learning in their developing brains (De Bellis and Zisk 2014).

The effects of trauma and stress are further exacerbated by living in communities that are ever more disconnected. We know that secure, responsive relationships with caring adults form the foundation for early cognition. Parenting originally took place in multigenerational clans where other adults and even older children would have taken the baby when the mother needed a break and provided a buffer to the parent-child relationship. The nuclear family unit, consisting of one or two parents caring for children, is a far cry from the way we evolved to raise children. Further, many Latin American, Asian, African, Middle Eastern, and Slavic cultures tend to emphasize a collectivist worldview grounded in relationships, interdependence, and community. Families with their roots in these cultures are more hardwired to favor a communal view of the world (Hammond 2015). Our US society has pulled away from the communities that have supported families for generations. While the past was far from idyllic for most BIPOC families in the United States, the challenges we face have been worsened in some respects over the past decades because of the decline of social support that buffered the stress for families. For example, families have become more disconnected with the rise of technology and with the trend of young adults moving farther away from their families of origin.

These are the social structures in which we are tasked with bringing up young humans. As a previously unwed mother and educator, I am all too aware of the factors working against us. I've read *ad nauseam* about how the stressors we face as a Black family living in a rural community, barely above the poverty line, will affect my child's development.

I can't change the social structures that are part of the fabric of our country, but I can take a walk outside with my son and invite others to join us.

While attending the Miami Herbert Business School at the University of Miami, I was among a handful of students in my class invited to join the nascent Bermont Carlin Scholar program. This program was for the top students in my class who would receive specialized Wall Street prep training and be flown to New York to meet the top investment firms. Through this opportunity, I landed an internship in the summer before my senior year and a job offer at one of the top wealth management firms in the country before I graduated with my bachelor's degree in business administration. I was excited to start my career working in finance in New York City! As a high-performing student my whole life, this job felt like the award at the end of the race. I joined a class of about twenty analysts in a two-year program and learned about finance and investing while traveling the country and meeting high-profile individuals. During my five years at the firm, I kept having this nagging sense that I was supposed to be happy. I got the job, I had the salary, I was traveling the country, and I was meeting celebrities; yet I still felt this flame of light within me slowly dimming.

And that is when I had the pleasure of meeting the inspiring founder of an outdoor democratic learning center in New York City. I first encountered this wonderful learning community at a farmers market in Harlem. Discovering this unique learning center and its alternative, outside-of-the-box view of education, as well as its view of childhood in general, set that flickering flame within me ablaze. My mind began to slowly open as questions that had remained dormant pushed to the surface. What is education? Why is our school system the way that it is? What if it were something different? What if learning could be pleasurable and *fun*? What if we all had a light within us? What if that light didn't have to fade? What if there is more to life than money and prestige?

I felt like I was awakening, and I was compelled to find the answers to those questions. I noticed the school needed volunteers, and although I wasn't sure what a financial analyst could offer a school, the school founder serenely welcomed me into the community. I did a few odd marketing jobs for the school, and in that time, I witnessed children of five years old who were well spoken, calm, and most importantly had a light in their eyes. They seemed to hum with excitement as they went about creating a comic strip and having a community discussion about how to be a good friend. I started to remember my own excitement as a young person in school, but as I flashed forward through the memories of my school career, I recalled how the excitement had slowly started to fade as reading became a means to pass a test or write a paper and

Walking along the path holding hands

math became a source of shame when I failed to keep pace in calculus. The joy of learning had transmuted into a pursuit of accomplishment and competition. My self-worth was inextricably tied into that chase, and my self-knowing suffered. As I sat in my cubicle reflecting on all this, four years into my career in financial services, I started to cry.

I realized in that moment that I no longer knew who I was, and I could no longer sense what I even wanted. I lamented how my own education had left me feeling stripped of my connection with my inner being. I remembered that my first career choice had been teaching. It was then that I decided to move back home to Florida and dive headfirst into a career change.

I started my teaching career as a Teach for America corps member in Jacksonville, Florida, where I experienced firsthand modern-day segregation in education. Over sixty years after *Brown v. Board of Education,* I found myself assigned to a school that was over 92 percent black and 81 percent low-income, where only 17 percent of students earned a passing score on the state reading test. Our school day was strictly regulated, with frequent visits from the State Department of Education aimed at "turning around" our school. State standards had to be written verbatim on the board, then again as an "I can . . ." statement, and then had to be repeated by students to demonstrate that learning was taking place. Blocks of at least ninety minutes each were devoted to reading and math, a routine that was strictly enforced, with a tolerance for some science instruction throughout the day. We were allowed no more than fifteen minutes of recess, the outdoor time my students not only craved but badly needed.

In retrospect, it might be fair to say that the school day felt like jail time for students and teachers alike. As a brand-new educator, I did not have the education, experience, or research-based knowledge that I have accumulated in the years since to understand just how badly my students needed to move. My students needed real experiences. My students needed fresh air! But instead, this natural need was used like a weapon. Movement and outdoor time were granted only as a reward for "good behavior" in exchange for the very human need to feel connected with one's body and with the natural world. Further, keeping students locked away in the classroom reinforced the negative self-belief in students that they were "bad," and that only "good" children could play outside.

It quickly became clear to me that this was neither a successful nor pleasurable learning experience. While we were spoon-fed all the latest research on what to do in the classroom to "reach our students," none of it seemed to be working. We were failing these children. We were robbing them of the pleasure of learning by forcing down their throats an approach to learning that was not made for them. We pressured them to read and interpret words on a page without providing opportunities for them to have real experiences.

Students observing the life cycle of the monarch butterfly

In that first year, I had an opportunity to go beyond the text in a science lesson on weathering and erosion. I lugged a fifty-pound bag of sand to school that day and snuck my students to the playground outside of our allotted time. The students poured water on the sand and observed how the water eroded their sand piles. They watched as the wind weathered their piles. They recorded their observations while the Florida sunshine warmed their brown skin. That day, even my most reluctant learners diligently jotted notes in their observation journals or verbally shared with me their learnings.

Shortly after this experience, the school determined that not enough time was being spent in reading. Our science time was shortened in favor of more time spent on small group reading and personalized technology activities. While I did not get many opportunities to experience nature education in my two years at that school again, these few experiences left a lasting impression that showed me how nature and real experiences could *really* reach our students.

In the throes of my second turbulent year teaching, I found out I was pregnant. I had a renewed sense of urgency to find the answers to my questions about what education really is. I drew back to the awakening I experienced in New York, diving deeper into the research surrounding early childhood education and development. I was intrigued by the nature-based preschools in Europe and the growing movement in the United States, as well as the work of Maria Montessori.

After having my son in 2019, I started working at a Montessori charter school. During that time, I grew more interested in whole child education and the role nature plays in that education. At the charter school I learned about "freedom within limits" and witnessed how trusting in students to guide their own education led to happier students and teachers and greater academic achievements. While working at the charter felt like a breath of fresh air after my first teaching experience, there was still a nagging feeling that we could be doing more. So, in 2020 an idea was born: a Montessori microschool in our community founded on the principles of being nature based, community embedded, and equity driven, led by teachers, not administrators. We reached out to the Wildflower network of schools and began to create Blazing Stars Montessori School, a place where we could bring joy and wonder back into education, specifically for the young boys of color in our community. Our school now has 64 percent BIPOC children, compared to Dade City, which is 47 percent BIPOC. The families we serve in our school are 75 percent very low- to middle-income families.

The harvest of sweet potatoes

Planting day

Knowing that a big part of our joy and wonder comes from nature and play-based learning, I worked to complete my Level 1 training for nature-based education through the Eastern Region Association for Forest and Nature Schools. I also continued studying the work of organizations such as Tinkergarten to explore how I could bring this type of education to our microschool.

Exploring trees

Most of the schools and child care centers in our area offer only 20 to 30 minutes of outdoor time to satisfy the state's legal requirement. But at Blazing Stars we have anywhere from 60 to 120 minutes a day of unstructured outdoor time. When we first opened our doors in a former child care facility, our playground was very simple, yet our children created a range of experiences for themselves that kept them engaged even in the blistering Florida heat.

One spring the children were fascinated by caterpillars and then became curious when all the caterpillars disappeared! This led to a whole unit on the life cycle of different insects. They have found seeds dropped from trees and wondered about roots and how plants grow. They have compared the soil of compost versus our native sand. They have invented group games involving all the students, a group composed of children aged three to six years of diverse socioeconomic and racial backgrounds. They work on social-emotional skills, including conflict resolution, self-advocacy, and anger management. Our students are the ones whose social and emotional needs tend to get overlooked in the traditional education system, but we find that within a few weeks at our program, the children become more regulated and peaceful in our environment.

In addition to the generous amount of free time and outdoor play, we have also started "Forest Fridays," when we spend half of the day outside at a county park. When new students come into our community, one of the first things our students are excited to share with them is the day we get to spend outside in the forest! We also enjoy "Gardening with Grands," when grandparents join us during the Florida growing seasons in spring and fall to tend our garden. We ask parents and siblings to join us as an extended family, so our families get to build relationships with the others in our community. Our hope is that these connections will help buffer the stresses of everyday life and build a network of support for the children in our care. Parents have anecdotally shared that these are not experiences they have had in other settings, and they enjoy learning alongside their children while building relationships with the other parents in our school community. In a time when community and trust for one's neighbors seem so out of reach, I am proud to be a part of a community built in mutual trust through nature-based education and a shared belief in the power of children to create a better world.

Reflection Questions

1. What are the implications for equity when some students are allowed to play outside for "good" behavior and other are kept indoors for "bad" behavior?
2. What are some ways that nature and outdoor learning help children retain their excitement for learning, allowing them to take their joy with them throughout their educational journey?
3. "Forest Fridays" provide a great way for schools to dedicate one day every week to taking students outside. A local park can serve as the "forest" in urban environments. What are some potential challenges you foresee in implementing this idea, and how can you overcome those challenges?
4. Do you agree with the author that "it's easier to step outside than it is to change social structures"? Why or why not?
5. In what ways is going outside an act of resistance?

References

De Bellis, Michael D., and Abigail Zisk. 2014. "The Biological Effects of Childhood Trauma." *Child and Adolescent Psychiatric Clinics of North America* 23 (2). https://pmc.ncbi.nlm.nih.gov/articles/PMC3968319/.

Ely, Danielle M., and Anne K. Driscoll. 2023. "Infant Mortality in the United States, 2021: Data from the Period Linked Birth/Infant Death File." *National Vital Statistics Reports* 72 (11). www.cdc.gov/nchs/data/nvsr/nvsr72/nvsr72-11.pdf.

Hammond, Zaretta. 2015. *Culturally Responsive Teaching and the Brain: Promoting Authentic Engagement and Rigor Among Culturally and Linguistically Diverse Students.* Corwin Press.

Hoyert, Donna L. 2023. "Maternal Mortality Rates in the United States, 2021." National Center for Health Statistics. https://dx.doi.org/10.15620/cdc:124678.

Maté, Gabor, and Daniel Maté. 2023. *The Myth of Normal: Trauma, Illness and Healing in a Toxic Culture.* Vintage Canada. Ebook.

CHAPTER 3

Bridging the Nature Gap for BIPOC Children

Lotus Chaney, Chattanooga, TN

Lotus Chaney describes herself as "a nature woman, a global citizen, and a habitual eater of food." She is mama to her son Ren and wife and best friend to her partner, Jophyel. An environmental researcher with more than twelve years of experience in the field and a lifetime of experience playing outside, Lotus is also a farmer, food science educator, Master Gardener, sustainable finance enthusiast, agroecologist, outdoor classroom specialist, food literacy educator, conference speaker, and homeschooler. Her personal projects include using action research to explore the concept of epigenetics through immersion in nature and healthy relationships with nutritious food.

I CONSIDER MYSELF A medical refugee. Since I chose to give birth in Costa Rica because of the record-high maternal mortality rates in Georgia, I have resisted becoming a statistic. I've also created a radical educational experience for my son Ren through global citizenship, daily nature immersion, the problem-posing educational model, Montessori-inspired teachings, and unbridled imagination. Before his conception, my experiences with nature and education had already solidified my commitment to creating a unique path for my son. For the first two years of his life, I've had the privilege and strength to make sure he doesn't become just another number in the United States. He's now a global resident, a dual citizen who speaks three languages. Ren is fully immersed in multicultural experiences, connected to natural spaces, and free to explore every angle of his environment.

This story follows Ren's adventures hiking a volcano in Costa Rica, camping with wolves, having a tantrum in a cloud forest, rock climbing on the roof of a building, taking countless plane rides, feeding giraffes, watching a total lunar eclipse, and more—all before the age of three. The story also shares how I've successfully integrated ideas from epigenetics and alternative education into nature play and my parenting/teaching.

As philanthropist Robert F. Smith's (2022) organization describes it, the "nature gap" is "a combination of racial and economic disparities that directly affect the well-being of communities of color, especially Black, Asian, Hispanic, and Latino communities." Historically, there have been many barriers to nature for us, including racial discrimination (Landau et al. 2020); stereotypes of nature and who belongs in it (Humphrey 2020); and limited physical access to natural/green spaces due to a lack of proximity and/or transportation. This lack is intertwined with health barriers, as Black children and families are more likely to have health issues that are exacerbated by environmental factors, like asthma and allergies, primarily because they are also overwhelmingly more exposed to ecological pollution than are White people. BIPOC communities are more likely to be ravaged by human modification (Theobald et al. 2020), as land within and surrounding them is taken for highways, power plants, construction sites (Tabuchi and Popovich 2021), dams, chemical plants, oil refineries, and more. Black people, specifically, are also 58 percent more likely than White people to live in nature-deprived communities; this is true across the United States and true for most forms of nature, including wetlands, forests, and even streams (Landau et al. 2020). This gap between BIPOC populations and everyone else has both currently and historically affected us in multiple ways, including mentally, emotionally, and spiritually.

Lack of exposure to nature due to segregation and systemic racism means less representation that allows us to see ourselves in nature, which creates the belief that we don't belong there or that we are separated from nature; often, because of this, we don't go in nature. And so, the cycle continues.

The nature gap materialized for me while I was teaching Farm to Early Childhood Education (ECE) in Georgia. I moved from Los Angeles to metro Atlanta in 2015 to join a service term with FoodCorps. I was especially interested in working with early learners and landed an internship with an early child care center that pioneered Farm to Early Childhood Education. This child care center, serving primarily Black and Latino students, was located in a deep inner city with no green spaces, few grocery stores, and long-standing car pollution. In this space, I saw the children's excitement about interacting with nature, digging in dirt, examining worms, planting seeds, and testing soil but realized the parents and caregivers felt a disconnect. Having moved from Los Angeles, home of many health nuts, to me this juxtaposition was new. I had a lot to learn about the unique relationships between people, nature, and food in the South. It was a culture shock to experience a place where going into natural spaces like hiking trails, national parks, or any heavily wooded area could be life-threatening for some Black people. I learned more about the birth, growth, and importance of soul food in the South. I experienced different cultures that are connected to the land, like the Gullah Geechee, and learned how White people had actively reduced these ancestral connections or nearly eradicated them through urbanization, segregation, and even climate change.

During this time in Atlanta in 2015, I understood how this nature gap could affect future generations, but I also felt immense hope and accomplishment as a Farm to ECE teacher there. I saw just how important my role was in facilitating the discovery and exploration of nature and nature play in communities where people looked like me. I saw myself in a unique position; from childhood, I had been deeply connected to nature, and as an Outdoor Classroom Specialist, I had a deep understanding of the concept of nature play and its importance in child development. Now I was able to leverage this knowledge and experience to help guide people to connect or reconnect with nature.

As stated in a report by the Center for American Progress, "No age group needs nature more than children. Studies consistently find that children who spend time outdoors in natural environments experience improved health and cognitive functions, strong motor coordination, reduced stress, and enhanced social skills" (Rowland-Shea et al. 2020). Nature play is one of the easiest ways to increase BIPOC children's outdoor exposure. However, for children to play in nature, they must have access to nature. Luckily, there are quite a few ways to facilitate this.

We can all infuse green spaces into our communities, apartments, schools, and backyards. Neighborhoods are transforming with urban food forests, community gardens, increasing tree canopy, and schoolyard forests. Still, houseplants, fresh flowers, and even worm farms can create meaningful connections to nature for children.

Access to nature is a critical issue for communities of color in the United States. People of color often do not feel welcomed or safe in parks or other natural areas due to the systemic and historical racism around public nature spaces. From the inception of the National Park Service, Black people were legally barred from entering these natural areas and others around the country. Through the hard, and often dangerous, work of Black and Brown freedom fighters, public outdoor spaces are now available to everyone, but that has not erased the memory and fear of exclusion for people of color. As KangJae "Jerry" Lee, a social and environmental justice researcher, put it, "Outdoor spaces weren't just coded as White, they were White. They were defined and managed as White spaces" (Asmelash 2021). This is a historical truth that must be acknowledged when working with children and families of color in outdoor education. While large, public natural areas are one space for connecting to nature, research by David Sobel and Julie Ernst (2023) found that children in programs with some nature-based learning reaped the same benefits for their executive functioning skills as children in programs that were predominantly outdoors. While we must continue to strive to provide our children and families of color with frequent access to nature, this finding by Sobel and Ernst can help urban-based outdoor educators feel heartened that any access they can provide is impactful.

Despite all this, a lack of representation will often fracture children's relationship with nature. In the short term, children may think these places aren't for them, that they don't belong there, or even that they are unsafe. In the long term, children may see themselves as separate from nature, a mindset that can influence behaviors and actions regarding climate change and environmental stewardship. Children with this perspective grow into adults who believe climate change doesn't affect them; since they don't go in nature, there is no incentive to protect it. This perspective is so prevalent today that Robert M. Pyle, famed author and ecologist, coined the phrase "the extinction of experience" (Soga and Gaston 2016). This phrase represents a phenomenon in which, through urban development and the growth of cities, the citizens (including children) grow more removed from personal contact with nature. This mindset is especially dangerous for the BIPOC children who come from communities that are most heavily influenced by environmental racism, including long-term air, water, and soil pollution.

Alternatively, if you see nature as a safe place, you'll retreat there for solace and stress relief. As the stresses of daily life pile up, it's been shown that creating green spaces in BIPOC communities decreases violence, including gun violence and burglary (Branas et al. 2018). The community views these green spaces as places for socializing and relaxing, which suggests they may increase mental well-being, which can be described as realizing your potential, coping well with everyday stressors, and flourishing mentally (Houlden et al. 2018)—precisely what we all want for children. This is especially true for children who have or continue to experience toxic stress, which can be caused by extreme poverty or unsafe living conditions, and which can manifest into both mental and physical conditions in their adult lives.

The problem-posing educational model heavily influenced my teaching and parenting philosophy. In my collaborative approach to learning, no one party holds all the knowledge because problem-posing learning is a collective process that incorporates the personal experiences of "learners" to solve a problem, explore a new concept, or answer a question. This model also leans heavily on introducing and developing liberation and social awareness tools. Utilizing this model, I found outdoor education to be a fantastic environment that allowed the constant flow of knowledge between all parties, and it was one of the best places to observe different perspectives at play. This educational model worked just as well during my time working with children growing and eating food. Food has such a cultural significance, even from a young age, that the flow of knowledge is natural when it is included in the curriculum. In my class, this looked like anything from crafting a cookbook for children's favorite foods to discovering the best way to water tomatoes.

I also began using action research at the child care center in Georgia to help build the Farm to ECE movement in Atlanta, and I quickly found my voice as a conference speaker. My research included introducing the concept of nutrition education to inner city ECE environments to combat multigenerational public health disparities like diabetes and heart disease. I had the pleasure of showcasing concrete evidence of its importance and real-life examples of how it's done at my first conference in 2015. Throughout my time there I increased my expertise in family nutrition and promoted cooking with children to increase self-confidence, relieve stress, improve math and reading skills, and create stronger bonds (Garcia et al. 2020), much as time in nature can. Soon my conference résumé grew, and I expanded nationwide.

Interestingly enough, at the same time as I experienced this nature gap, I also had my first real encounter with racism and intentional exclusion from professional opportunities in the environmental space. After my FoodCorps term, I watched as my other cohort members got hired as school garden educators or program staff, yet there I sat with over four years of experience and I couldn't even get an internship with any of the significant "Good Food" folks around the city. I soon realized that I (the only Black person in the group) had essentially been blacklisted by my cohort supervisor (a White woman with deep roots in the community) after I challenged her authority. I grew up in Inglewood, California, and I have no issues having "difficult" conversations—I don't take no sh*t. After talking with inside parties, I discovered she had intentionally made my FoodCorps term as tricky as possible. This meant I taught at three schools located in opposite directions, each nearly two hours from my house, even though I was the only service member without personal transportation. Luckily, through a personal connection with the school director at Little Ones Learning Center, I was soon offered an internship.

Fast-forward to 2020, the year we'll all remember. I wanted to start a family but was wrestling with the idea of being a stay-at-home mom or continuing to pursue this work. I also taught gardening to an even younger age group, eighteen-month-olds, at a new early child care center. My daily interactions with boundless childhood wonder in the outdoors solidified my desire to make nature-based learning a permanent part of my life, even after I became a mom.

Around the same time as I was planning my pregnancy, the country saw the eruption of the Black Lives Matter movement amid the continuation of hostility toward Black lives. I also understood what this context could mean for my unborn baby and their right to a safe future as a Black person. As the researcher I am, I heavily investigated the statistics: because I lived in the South, I was surrounded by the highest maternal mortality rates in the country. With Georgia near the top of the list, I was confronted with another decision: What did I want my birthing experience to be like? I spent countless hours reading home birth materials and dissecting the research behind home births and positive birthing experiences. I analyzed the risks of this choice, investigated how it's different for Black women, and looked into every alternative available to me. The birthing center was too expensive, and the hospital wasn't an option for me. I made my choice to have a home birth, and next I had to decide where to do it.

Our decision to give birth in Costa Rica was heavily influenced by genetics, specifically epigenetics. Epigenetics studies change in organisms caused by the modification of gene expression rather than changes to the genetic code itself. In other words, it is the study of how behaviors and the environment cause changes that affect how genes work.

Now seems like a good time to mention that another reason why I became so passionately interested in nutrition education was because both my maternal and paternal family trees have a long history of diet-related diseases and cancer. This includes everything from high blood pressure, diabetes, obesity, heart disease, and kidney failure to complex gastrointestinal issues. I also had a near-death experience in high school because I was making diet-related decisions without any proper nutrition education. As of February 2023, there were no federal requirements for nutrition education in public or private schools, a missed opportunity to create positive physical and societal outcomes, including short- and long-term healthy eating, undernutrition prevention, improved academic attendance, behavior, and achievement, and decreased overall diet-related health care costs (Association of State Public Health Nutritionists 2024). Not only this, but doctors receive less than twenty hours of nutrition education in medical school (Adams et al. 2010), meaning they cannot confidently talk about dietary solutions for health. However, good nutrition can prevent more than 11 million diet-related deaths annually (Afshin et al. 2019).

Understanding epigenetics is crucial because it heavily influences how I teach others and parent my son. If I can create the right environment, physical and otherwise, for him, I can change how his DNA is fundamentally designed to work. So, for me, cocreating a nature-infused childhood for Ren means more than appreciating sensory-rich memories, vibrant cultures, and nourishing foods; it's about giving him the tools to save his own life. It's about freeing him from ignorance that can quickly become a death sentence. So, what does that look like for us?

Since August 2021, Ren has spent much time outdoors, surrounded by nature and birdsong. He received his first passport when he was eight weeks old and is a dual citizen. Straight out of the womb, he spent most of his newborn stage in the fresh air. Our windows were open during his birth as the rainy breeze comforted my tired body. A few days after he was born, I watched my postpartum anxiety develop as his little body turned yellow from jaundice. My midwife prescribed daily walks in the morning mountain sun instead of traditional phototherapy in a tank. After about three months in Costa Rica, we returned to the United States, and it was finally time for the rest of our family to meet him. It was the winter of 2021, so spending lots of time outside wasn't as easy, but I found that taking in "sips" of the cold Georgia air helped ease my postpartum hormones. In the spring, we took more steps outside. It felt like we were emerging anew; we were almost reborn.

Back in November 2020, I had become a founding member of a hyperlocal urban farm in metro Atlanta, and when I returned from giving birth, the farm once again became a place of healing for me. I put my hands in the dirt and made meals with fresh produce grown by those I knew and trusted. I brought my nephew there to experience a little taste of farm life as we harvested collard greens and played with the goats. I was overjoyed when Ren turned six months old and I could finally start baby-led weaning with organic vegetables from the farm, now known as Unearthing Farm and Market.

Farms soon became a favorite place for us, and rightfully so. As I write this, we've been to eight farms across the South before his third birthday. My personal favorites were the pumpkin patch at Flat Top Mountain Farm in Soddy-Daisy, Tennessee, and Southern Belle Farm in McDonough, Georgia, where we've gone strawberry and peach picking and adventured through a massive ocean of zinnias and sunflowers in the middle of a southern July.

My son, Ren, at Flat Top Mountain

Traversing Jardín Else Kientzler, a seventeen-acre botanical garden at the top of the slopes of Costa Rica's Central Mountain Range

Outside of building a healthy connection with nature and food, we also prioritize cultural diversity for Ren. We found the best way to do this was to embrace global citizenship. I grew up in a melting-pot community, and interacting with different cultures and backgrounds has greatly enriched my life. In middle school, I became especially interested in Costa Rica. As a country where 95 to 98 percent of its electricity has come from renewable sources since 2014 and that closed all its zoos in 2013, it ticked all the boxes for me and soon for my husband, Jophyel, too. Its Caribbean coast is also home to cultures of African descent, making it a haven of sorts for Black expatriates from the United States.

When I was five months pregnant, my husband and I visited Costa Rica for the first time. It instantly felt like home, and we basked in the warmth of the national motto, *pura vida*, which means "pure life." We moved there full-time shortly after Ren turned eighteen months old. Free from the stress and fear of police brutality, toxic productivity, and living a performative life, *pure* life is precisely what we felt.

We explored, adventured, and thrived for the next five months while fully immersed in jungle living. We stayed in tiny cottages with green geckos, enjoying home-cooked meals from neighbors. During our time there, my family and I joined a community of other Black expats who wanted a beautiful place to exist. Some were families with small children who saw value in multicultural communities and cherished the opportunity to live in this small but incredibly ecologically diverse Central American country. We shared stories of the immense peace and love we felt there, and how those things were almost instantly disrupted once we stepped back onto US soil.

My favorite memory was when Ren became captivated by volcanoes, so naturally we visited one. At Poás Volcano National Park, we touched leaves as large as our bodies, heard the cries of scarlet macaws in the distance, and hiked up to the fog-blanketed blue lagoon at the summit.

Next, our friend drove us down to the local waterfall park. It was exhilarating as we stepped behind the 121-foot La Paz waterfall together, listening to the monkeys overhead and relishing the power of water. This is a moment I will remember forever, and I hope Ren will too.

At the end of our time living in Costa Rica, we settled in Chattanooga, minutes from the Tennessee River. Field trips have been a significant part of our lives as I've continued to use action research while homeschooling my toddler. This research has included exploring the biophilia hypothesis, which considers

Ren on top of Poás Volcano

La Paz waterfall

the possibility of "an innate biological and genetic connection between human and nature, including an emotional dimension to this connection," through a combination of nature-based education, world schooling, and Montessori teaching principles (Gaekwad et al. 2022). In harmony with Montessori teaching principles, these trips are mostly child-directed and let us conduct field research on our weekly themes.

As I am a working toddler mom, having structure is vital for our family. I have curated a "prepared environment," a Montessori concept that features a calm and structured learning place where children generally know what to expect. In our home, an eight-cube organizer anchors this environment. Ren has free and unrestricted access to this prepared environment all day. This organizer contains themed materials, such as coloring pages, wooden spoons, animal figurines, and so on. These materials are grouped by theme, and I choose a different theme each week that corresponds with a physical place, often our "field trip." For example, we'll visit the aquarium or the Tennessee River during water week, and during bug week, we hike or look under rocks outside. We typically visit this place at the end of the workweek or on the weekend. This has been the best way for us to explore topics Ren is interested in through books, experiments, activities, and physical exploration.

We even had a camping week that culminated with an overnight stay at a nature preserve at the top of the notoriously racist Lookout Mountain. I use the term "notoriously racist" for the mountain because of the history of racial discrimination and violence tied to Lookout Mountain and the surrounding area. Of course, the mountain itself isn't capable of racism, but it has long been a site of historical oppression and injustice. For example, during the Civil War, Confederate soldiers used the mountain as a lookout point. Later on it became a gathering spot for segregationist groups who adopted it as a symbol of White supremacy. This was a full-circle moment as my husband and son camped outside for the first time, as I had done so often as a child. The moment felt even more robust and beautiful when my husband woke up in the darkness, seemingly alarmed at the sound of red wolves howling in the nearby rehabilitation habitat. My words to him were, "Baby, go back to sleep; you're safe." All I've ever wanted was to give him and Ren that safety.

Since Ren's birth, I've worked to make him feel comfortable in natural and green spaces. Nature is where we eat our favorite foods, play our favorite games, and go with our favorite people, all to promote positive memories, create representation, and foster healthy relationships with the outdoors. I strive to give Ren constant and (mostly) unrestricted exploration of natural spaces daily. Before he turned one, this meant spending most days outside on the porch. From eighteen months of age and beyond, Ren began playing with me near

Ren and author at Reflection Riding Nature Preserve

the shore of the Tennessee River, where he started with supervised risky play, like climbing trees, inspecting beneficial insects, running at high speed, and rough-and-tumble play. Risky play has been shown to give children the chance to learn resilience, negotiation skills, independence, and even self-regulation (Spencer et al. 2021).

I've seen countless benefits of nature play and how they're manifesting in Ren's development. Some of these have included behavioral changes, especially in toddlerhood, as we've used natural spaces to regulate big emotions. Outdoors Ren has learned spatial awareness through unique opportunities for fine- and gross-motor skill development. While we lived in Costa Rica, nature was a place for bilingual language development. We've also used nature play in many other ways: to guide STEM education; to allow structured and unstructured interactions with animals; to teach about geography, insects, plants, and earth systems like earthquakes and rain showers; to pursue ecological exploration by visiting rainforests, volcanos, forests, nature reserves, sanctuaries, zoos, and aquariums; and to foster healthy social interactions both in Costa Rica and in the United States.

Nature has been a positive anchor all my life. I know my love connection with the earth started long before I was born, somewhere, somehow. This connection has guided most, if not all, of my decisions in life. Because I've had so many positive experiences with the natural world, I can accurately articulate its importance in my success and my path in life, from my likes and dislikes to my morals and values to my career and parenting style.

Ren on the Tennessee River

Multiple times in this chapter, I've talked about how I want to create an impact, so let me tell you what I've come up with: I am composing meaningful connections with nature for all, but especially for BIPOC children, and over the twelve years I've been obsessed, I've found a few ways to do this. Between 2015 and 2024, I spoke at ten conferences, sharing my expertise on child and family nutrition, creating food sovereignty in communities through environmental education, and exploring food science with early learners. This has allowed me to create reach, resources, and peer learning around the world for all those interested in creating, fostering, and sustaining greater relationships with nature in their own communities. I start with family and friends while continuing to create space for other BIPOC folks who are curious about getting outside. For me, this includes finding free and low-cost outside experiences that provide low-barrier, engaging opportunities to explore our local areas.

I don't think there is one single solution that can begin to dismantle the barriers riddling BIPOC communities regarding nature access and nature play. Historically, activists have worked on creating more representation and improving access to national parks and hiking trails, and this work is valid and necessary—but it is not enough. It's going to take a multitude of ideas to solve a variety of problems. I have continued to work with community movers and shakers to facilitate climate-centered city and business partnerships globally, to create stability and liberation for Black farmers, and to accelerate conversations with conservation leadership nationwide. As I look to the future, I plan to study landscape architecture and permaculture while incorporating my skills as a Master Gardener to create more holistic nature-based solutions in Black communities.

It's clear to me that there should be more emphasis on cleaning up pollution in BIPOC neighborhoods because, frankly, pollution is killing Black folks

(Villarosa 2020), and that issue needs to be solved. We're in a particular time where climate-related matters are at the forefront for many people, especially as we experience record heat and as post-COVID conversations and trends have created more outdoor engagement and interest. These factors created a pathway for the passing of the Inflation Reduction Act of 2022, which included the most significant financial investment in climate action in US history. The legislation provided for multibillion-dollar funding of energy and climate change initiatives, with 40 percent of the money designated for socially disadvantaged communities (the bulk of which are BIPOC communities), providing a unique opportunity for more local governments to help scale the "just transition." The term *just transition* was used in the 1980s by US trade unions aiming to protect workers whose jobs were affected by air and water pollution regulations, but the concept has now evolved into an environmental movement describing a transition to a low-carbon economy with no one left behind. This investment has the potential to create significant climate action through incentives for local governments to incorporate nature-based solutions into city planning and neighborhood infrastructure.

What are nature-based solutions, you ask? Nature-based solutions, or NbS, utilize natural systems and principles to solve climate, economic, and social issues. NbS are dynamic and holistic; they can simultaneously influence climate change, water security, water pollution, food security, human health, biodiversity loss, disaster risk management, and more. Using nature to solve problems is more cost-effective (Pearce 2022) and creates faster returns than built or engineered solutions, also called gray infrastructure. This is especially true concerning environmental issues many cities struggle with, such as the phenomenon of heat islands, which are urban areas where buildings and roads trap and reflect heat, causing unusually high temperatures. NbS can address this and other problems, making cities better places to live and work.

In BIPOC communities, relationships are vital to creating sustainable change. This is true because of the overbearing and underperforming nature of work done in these communities by White saviorism, especially in the nonprofit space, with the result that trust is at a premium. BIPOC people and the communities they live in have been test subjects for everything from extractive research practices to culturally inappropriate programs and services that create paternalism and shame-based identities. Modeling programs to include NbS can help create those necessary relationships and increase trust, precisely because they are designed to be community led. Who doesn't want to live in a more beautiful place with clean air, soil, and water?

I believe that investing in NbS, especially in BIPOC communities, creates a bright future for accessible and beneficial nature play for the children who live

Ren looking at sunset

there. When it comes to what the future of nature play looks like for our son, I hope that when Ren looks all around him, he is surrounded by nature. I hope that at the same time, he is surrounded by the love, safety, and wonder that I felt as a child and that I continue to feel today. Lastly, I hope that when he looks to the horizon, he chooses to also compose impactful experiences in nature for the people he loves.

Reflection Questions

1. What are some of your earliest memories of playing in nature?
2. How has nature affected your life and well-being? How about the people around you?
3. What are some of the challenges that BIPOC communities near you face when it comes to accessing nature?
4. How can you encourage more place-based education in your teaching practice?

5. Can you identify opportunities to create more multicultural connections for your students? Can any of these connections be facilitated or explored outdoors?

6. What do you think about the term *extinction of experience*, and how do you want to revive nature play for the youth you educate?

References

Adams, Kelly, Martin Kohlmeier, and Steven H. Zeisel. 2010. "Nutrition Education in US Medical Schools: Latest Update of a National Survey." *Academic Medicine: Journal of the Association of American Medical Colleges* 85 (9): 1537–42. https://doi.org/10.1097/ACM.0b013e3181eab71b.

Afshin, Ashkan, Patrick John Sur, Kairsten A. Fay, et al. 2019. "Health Effects of Dietary Risks in 195 Countries, 1990–2017: A Systematic Analysis for the Global Burden of Disease Study 2017." *The Lancet* 393 (10184): 1958–72. https://doi.org/10.1016/s0140-6736(19)30041-8.

Asmelash, Leah. 2021. "Outdoor Recreation Has Historically Excluded People of Color. That's Beginning to Change." CNN, December 14. www.cnn.com/2021/12/14/us/national-parks-history-racism-wellness-cec.

Association of State Public Health Nutritionists. 2024. "Nutrition Education in America's Schools: A Policy Brief." ASPHN. https://asphn.org.

Branas, Charles C., Eugenia South, Michelle C. Kondo, et al. 2018. "Citywide Cluster Randomized Trial to Restore Blighted Vacant Land and Its Effects on Violence, Crime, and Fear." *Proceedings of the National Academy of Sciences* 115 (12): 2946–51. https://doi.org/10.1073/pnas.1718503115.

Gaekwad, Jason S., Anahita Sal Moslehian, Phillip B Roös, and Arlene Walker. 2022. "A Meta-Analysis of Emotional Evidence for the Biophilia Hypothesis and Implications for Biophilic Design." *Frontiers in Psychology* 13: 750245. https://doi.org/10.3389/fpsyg.2022.750245.

Garcia, Ada L., Emma Brown, Tom Goodale, Mairi McLachlan, and Alison Parrett. 2020. "A Nursery-Based Cooking Skills Programme with Parents and Children Reduced Food Fussiness and Increased Willingness to Try Vegetables: A Quasi-Experimental Study." *Nutrients* 12 (9): 2623. https://doi.org/10.3390/nu12092623.

Houlden, Victoria, Scott Weich, João Porto de Albuquerque, Stephen Jarvis, and Karen Rees. 2018. "The Relationship Between Greenspace and the Mental Wellbeing of Adults: A Systematic Review." *PLOS ONE* 13 (9): e0203000. https://doi.org/10.1371/journal.pone.0203000.

Humphrey, Naomi. 2020. "Breaking Down the Lack of Diversity in Outdoor Spaces." National Health Foundation, July 20. https://nationalhealthfoundation.org/breaking-down-lack-diversity-outdoor-spaces.

Landau, Vincent A., Meredith L. McClure, and Brett G. Dickson. 2020. "Analysis of the Disparities in Nature Loss and Access to Nature." Conservation Science Partners,

May 29. www.csp-inc.org/public/CSP-CAP_Disparities_in_Nature_Loss_FINAL_Report_060120.pdf.

Pearce, Fred. 2022. "Why Are Nature-Based Solutions on Climate Being Overlooked?" *Yale Environment 360,* April 18. https://e360.yale.edu/features/why-are-nature-based-solutions-on-climate-being-overlooked.

Robert F. Smith Philanthropy. 2022. "Understanding the Nature Gap." Robert F. Smith Philanthropy, November 9. https://robertfsmith.org/news/the-access-to-nature-gap.

Rowland-Shea, Jenny, Sahir Doshi, Shanna Edberg, and Robert Fanger. 2020. "The Nature Gap: Confronting Racial and Economic Disparities in the Destruction and Protection of Nature in America." Center for American Progress, July 21. www.americanprogress.org/article/the-nature-gap.

Sobel, David, and Julie Ernst. 2023. "Some Nature Is Better Than No Nature: Bridging Research and Practice." *Exchange Press* 271, Fall. https://hub.exchangepress.com/articles-on-demand/19958/.

Soga, Masashi, and Kevin J. Gaston. 2016. "Extinction of Experience: The Loss of Human–Nature Interactions." *Frontiers in Ecology and the Environment* 14 (2): 94–101. https://doi.org/10.1002/fee.1225.

Spencer, Rebecca A., Nila Joshi, Karina Branje, Naomi Murray, Sara F. L. Kirk, and Michelle R. Stone. 2021. "Early Childhood Educator Perceptions of Risky Play in an Outdoor Loose Parts Intervention." *AIMS Public Health* 8 (2): 213–28. https://doi.org/10.3934/publichealth.2021017.

Stein, Marianne. 2023. "Soy Expansion in Brazil Linked to Increase in Childhood Leukemia Deaths." University of Illinois Urbana–Champaign College of Agricultural, Consumer & Environmental Sciences, October 23. https://aces.illinois.edu/news/soy-expansion-brazil-linked-increase-childhood-leukemia-deaths.

Tabuchi, Hiroko, and Nadja Popovich. 2021. "People of Color Breathe More Hazardous Air. The Sources Are Everywhere." *The New York Times,* April 28. www.nytimes.com/2021/04/28/climate/air-pollution-minorities.html.

Theobald, David M., Christina Kennedy, Bin Chen, James Oakleaf, Sharon Baruch-Mordo, and Joe Kiesecker. 2020. "Earth Transformed: Detailed Mapping of Global Human Modification from 1990 to 2017." *Earth System Science Data* 12 (3): 1953–72. https://doi.org/10.5194/essd-12-1953-2020.

Villarosa, Linda. 2020. "Pollution Is Killing Black Americans. This Community Fought Back." *The New York Times,* July 28. www.nytimes.com/2020/07/28/magazine/pollution-philadelphia-black-americans.html.

CHAPTER 4

Documentation as Conversation

Ron Grady, New Orleans, LA

Ron Grady is an educator, author, artist, and researcher whose work centers children's daily lives and experiences, emphasizing the beauty and depth of small moments through narrative, photography, and storytelling. He taught preschool at NOLA Nature School in New Orleans for many years and is now pursuing a PhD in education at Harvard.

He authored *Honoring the Moment in Young Children's Lives* and has a forthcoming book on photography with Redleaf Press. Additionally, he wrote and illustrated the children's books *What Does Brown Mean to You?* and *Beatrice Looks for Home* (both with Penguin). Ron also serves on the editorial board of *Voices of Practitioners*, the online journal of the National Association for the Education of Young Children.

My own journey to nature-based education was, put simply, an accident. During my first year as a preschool teacher in a play-based (yet indoor) classroom, my coteacher Karin came to me with a question. She shared that her friend Clare (who would later also become my friend) was planning to start a weekend nature-based program in a local park and she needed another person to facilitate it with her. Clare had originally asked Karin, but a scheduling conflict meant that Karin would no longer be able to work the program. Would I, Karin asked, be willing to help out? I gave an enthusiastic "Sure, why not!" with absolutely no clue of just how intensely that response would reverberate through my life. I helped Clare that first Saturday, and the next, and the next after that, and before we knew it, we were working together to bring her vision of nature-based education in the heart of New Orleans to life.

In this chapter, come with me to explore what it means to document children's experiences in natural worlds (and as members of natural worlds) for families. In particular, we will delve into what it can mean to maintain a sensitive awareness to the many ideas and ways of being that families bring to children's experiences in school generally and in nature schools specifically. This chapter begins by inviting us to consider, through families' lenses, the unique allures and challenges of nature-based early childhood settings. First, we consider the curiosities, concerns, and wonderings families might have. Then we look at how documentation might support us in responding to these concerns while, at the same time, continuing to advocate for children's right to play,

Children walking in the woods

to build meaningful relationships, and to create in collaborative communities. I encourage readers to reflect on the ways these principles may be broadly applied to family interactions, and to think about implementing these principles with pedagogies that are culturally sustaining and empowering (Paris and Alim 2007). I attempt to avoid making broad judgments here, acknowledging that the experiences explored herein are in a sense both universal and highly specific. Therefore, before you continue reading, I invite you to reflect on the following questions:

1. Who are your families?
2. What do they believe about nature?
3. What do you desire for your families to know about children? Childhood? Outdoor education?
4. What are the primary challenges you face in communicating with families about children's experiences? Where might you build on what is already in place communication-wise?
5. How, if at all, are the perspectives of the families in your program represented by dominant nature-based pedagogies or frameworks? In dominant conversations about documenting children's experiences? If they are not represented, what may be missing?
6. What might you and your program have the unique potential to add to the conversation?

Families and caregivers are central to children's experiences. As early educators, although the primary focus and priority of our daily work is children, we would be remiss if we exclude families and caregivers from the scope of our consideration. Indeed, for those of us who work in outdoor educational spaces where being in nature is a significant portion of our program, it is all the more important that we bring families into the fold. However, as we seek to do this, it is crucial that we consider: What brings families to our program in the first place?

If you ask someone to describe what nature-based education looks like, you'll likely get answers that touch on any variety of images: a ragtag group of children running barefoot through fields of flowers, adventuring up tall trees, moving through mud and muck with wide smiles, exploring the lives of plants and animals with intention—each child acquiring deep knowledge of, and affinity for, the natural world. These images hold powerful sway over popular imagination, and those of us who work with children outdoors know that these moments are, truly, a thousand times more beautiful to behold in real life than they are to imagine. These images, along with other ideas about what nature-based educational programs can do and how they can support children, tend to be significant draws for families. However, families may still have concerns.

Nature-based outdoor education for young children in many places still upends many of the familiar paradigms of school, preschool, and child care that we hold to as a society. These extant notions, furthermore, are often grounded in an old logic that current thought on education is increasingly interrogating, rejecting, and/or seeking to transform. Therefore, the time is ripe for novel ways of thinking.

The entire premise of this chapter is based on the understanding that acclimating parents and caregivers to what education looks like in a new paradigm is a critical piece of our work and perhaps the centerpiece of much of our documentation. Even those who opt their little ones into our programs often need support in their journeys as the parents and caregivers of children who spend their days outside. Our role as educators is to put aside our (valid) frustrations—after all, we might say, they did choose to be in this school! However, our job as educators is, as ever, to support children *and* their communities of care in feeling safe, welcome, seen, and genuinely part of the program. We are obligated to see and to respond to the children in our communities of creativity and care *and* to hold space for and dialogue with their caregiving communities. There is no more powerful way to invite caregivers into conversation than through documentation.

In my experience, documentation is one of the central ways we can support these families as they strive to develop comfort with their children's experiences of outdoor education. This idea, however, is far from novel, as chronicling children's experiences in school for families is part and parcel of many educational philosophies, approaches, and curricula. From the Reggio approach that encourages educators to thread together inquiry and aesthetics (Edwards et al. 2012; Wurm 2007) to prominent teaching frameworks and rating systems that rely on standardized scales and encourage the collection of a predetermined set of artifacts, there are many models for how to document children's work.

Defining Documentation

Documentation does not always look like a panel with a detailed mixture of text, photographs, reflection, and links to broader phenomena and frameworks. This model is ideal, but panels are constructed *over time*, not right away. Do not let the work involved in achieving this level of detail deter you from getting started.

Documentation can be messy, in-process, imperfect, and incomplete! It might involve one child or many; it can focus on a single phenomenon or a series of events or actions. A note sharing a single moment in a child's day can be meaningful documentation. You can connect this snapshot to broader themes using a single sentence or even key words or phrases (Stacey 2023).

Documentation is always intentional, illuminative, and constructed with a deep respect and love for children and their developmental and creative processes. It is a piece of communication in dialogue with children, colleagues, children's caregivers, and our broader community (Edwards et al. 2012; Grady 2024).

Documentation at its core is a conversation; it can both speak and respond to a number of questions, concerns, and curiosities that families have. Two of perhaps the most common concerns relate to safety and school readiness. Caregivers may ask: How can my child care for themselves and be safe outdoors? How will this time in nature, or in this nature-based setting, prepare my child for the academic rigors of school? In addition to addressing concerns, documentation can also be used to invite new ways of thinking. Where can we expand or extend our thinking about children and childhood?

Child with moss

Child splashing in the rain

Children climbing a tree

Response 1: Answering Concerns About Children's Ability to Care for Themselves and Be Safe

I asked a few nature-based educators I know to share the most common concerns parents and caregivers express in regard to outdoor learning. The cofounder and executive director of a Boston-area nature school wrote that parents often worry about their children being "outdoors in the cold and rain (and sometimes express the misconception that cold and rainy weather gives people colds)" (personal communication, October 2023). My good friend, nature educator and administrator Clare Loughran of NOLA Nature School, shared a related point, offering that when a parent has a concern, it "usually revolves around self-care." Among these concerns, Clare writes, are "worr[ies] about [things like] sunscreen application, hydration, bugs getting in lunch or lunch not staying cold. Sometimes," she adds, "we get parents worried about tree climbing or alligators, but that does seem less common" (personal communication, October 2023).

Caregivers want to know that, above all, children are being taken care of and feel able to seek out the help they need. While this is a common concern across all settings, when it takes place in nature, it adds a layer of unfamiliarity to which we must speak, ideally proactively. Stepping into our obligation as documenters of children's experiences involves showing how children respond to these challenges, for example, documenting what happens when a child feels cold or gets an insect bite.

You might ask these questions in framing your documentation:

- **How is a child responding to the weather? Does it bring them joy?**
- **What about when they are uncomfortable? How do they express it to you? How do you respond?**

Child with leaf

Response 2: Framing Documentation Based on (and Using Documentation to Push Back Against) Long-Standing Expectations About School

Brilliant leaves join an unseasonable warmth to lend an unusual atmosphere to this late October morning. I am visiting the Boston Outdoor Preschool Network where, today, the children are sharing a morning of reading with their families. I stand next to a wagon full of supplies as small groups of children snuggle up to parents and caregivers on soft blankets. One of the parents pours himself a cup of coffee, and we strike up a brief conversation. I ask him about his experiences at the school.

"We love this place," he tells me, adding, "but we're worried about her being the oldest next year."

I nod, and although I think I have an idea of what he might be getting at, I ask him, "Could you say a little more about your worry about her being the oldest? Is it an academic challenge sort of thing or . . ."

But before I finish the sentence, a wide smile breaks out across his face. We both know what he's getting at here. I share that his concern isn't one to take lightly, and that the reality is that moving between schools and spaces can be a difficult transition no matter what. The furrow of his brow and slow nod of his head suggests he's listening, but even still, he may not be wholly convinced.

An email exchange with the school's director suggested that this dad was far from alone. I asked the director what some of the common worries were for parents who enrolled their children in her school. "Will my child be prepared for kindergarten?" she wrote, calling it a "common" worry, related to "anxiety that their child's development is getting held back by the presence of younger children" (Sarah Besse, personal communication).

Anecdotes show us that despite families' affinity for our open-ended, child-directed program, there was almost universally some degree of concern over whether children would be what parents and caregivers referred to as "prepared." But, you might be thinking, aren't concerns about being prepared for *the subsequent year of schooling common across all years and types of school?* I would reply with a heartfelt "Yes!" You may, by now, start to notice a pattern! One of the most persistent concerns that the families of the children in all of my classes, nature and indoor, have expressed is related to their children's transition between years of schooling. However, as alluded to above, transitioning between nature-based and more traditional schools comes with additional dimensions of difference. Not only are nature-based schools (in contrast to many other educational contexts) often grounded in philosophies that center children's experiences within the arrangement of the curriculum itself, but the lived experience of being outside is very different from that of being inside. Any motion, for example, feels and looks different in expansive spaces. Sounds reverberate differently indoors than out. A chaotic moment in the forest can feel very different than a chaotic moment inside a four-walled room. People tend to have mental frameworks for one and not the other.

Therefore, for us, documenting has a multifaceted purpose. Not only do we need to demonstrate to families that children are developing the sorts of dispositions that might serve them well in school moving forward, but we also have to speak to—and push back against—unrealistic ideas about what children should be doing that are often, frankly, developmentally inappropriate for any child of the same age, whether in a nature school or not. We are documenting children's experiences, advocating for a new view, reassuring parents about children's development, and demonstrating a commitment to transparent accountability.

Child with colored glass

Children climbing a tree

Oliver and Mia are climbing a tree. Oliver is helping Mia figure out how to get through a tricky spot on the tree. Mia is stuck on a lower branch. Oliver waits for her, supremely unflappable in a situation where other children (and admittedly, I) might be consumed with impatience. The two have been climbing for nearly ten minutes. Oliver observes the situation, trying to figure out how to help Mia get past the tricky spot.

"OK, it looks like Mia is still stuck," he says, thinking aloud to himself. "Mia, the way I got out of there is . . . ," Oliver begins. However, midway through this sentence he seems to decide that showing will be better than telling. "Now watch me," he says. He hops over the branch where Mia is leaning and then, within seconds, ducks under it.

"Watch me, Mia, OK? I loopeded [sic] under."

"That's how I do it," Oliver adds. Mia has not yet moved.

Oliver is watching Mia as she leans over the branch. "You're trying to make it to the vines to here?"

"Yes."

"Oh, that's OK," he says, nodding. "Hey, Mia—I can see the whole airplane field!"

Mia gasps.

"Come up here, Mia, it's so high! I love this place."

"Whoa," Mia says as she pulls herself up the branch. She seems to be trying to lift her belly high enough to reduce the friction between her belly and the tree.

"Um, whoa. I'm climbing," she says. She has tried now, twice, to put both of her feet on the tree, foiled perhaps by fatigue and the heft of her boots.

Oliver has turned around again to look down at her. He watches for a second and says, "But you can't lift one of your feet up?"

Mia replies, "What?"

"You can't lift one of your feet up?" Oliver asks.

"So high," Mia says.

"High, you said?" Oliver replies.

"Yeah," she replies.

"Hey, hide like when you're playing hide-and-seek!" Oliver exclaims.

"And high," Mia says.

"'High' and 'hide'—they rhyme! When you're on a tree and you wanna go high, they rhyme! Hide and high! They rhy-y-yme!" Oliver singsongs.

How would you transform this snippet of interaction, recorded from less than a minute of a child's day, into something meaningful that can be interpreted by parents in ways they might expect? We can (1) explore what's happening, (2) connect this to traditional ideas about school, and (3) invite parents to consider where this fits into the children's experiences longer term. When doing this, I encourage you not to lose sight of the other core principles of documenting children's experiences.

So, what is actually happening here? Mia and Oliver are climbing a tree. Oliver makes it up quickly, while Mia takes more time. Neither child is agitated or frustrated, and Oliver repeatedly invites Mia to continue trying to climb up. He looks back at her, telling her about what's possible from the higher branch. He is also listening—listening to what Mia says, discerning her needs, and attending to her process while also thinking about what he would do if he were in her shoes.

How does this assessment connect to traditional ideas about school and what children do and learn there? The activity involves fine- and gross-motor skills, but there is more to be gained. The interaction demonstrates valuable social and emotional development and shows how the challenge of climbing trees is also an invitation into relationship and metacognition, providing an opportunity for children to see others' needs, experience friendship, and come to understand that we all need to try new things. Through his experience climbing the tree, Oliver also makes a connection to literacy and reveals his emerging ideas about words, sounds, rhymes, and more, providing a snapshot of his linguistic development as a four-year-old soon to be five. Such information might be especially valuable for caregivers interested in knowing how their child is progressing toward certain goals. Finally, we have to wonder: How can parents

Children climbing up the stairs

understand this scene more broadly in the context of human experience, rather than just in terms of concrete outcomes that will serve a child as they move between years at school? We might consider this method of taking documentation as playing "the long game." Often this term refers to conceding something that would be marginally more desirable in the short term (such as avoiding a scrape or a moment of fear) for long-term gain (a sense of accomplishment at having climbed and a foundational experience with and in nature). The metaphor and phrasing are imperfect, but the idea does begin to express some of what it could look like to be an advocate for children. Yes, we show parents that we are aware of their children's needs and their own desires as caregivers, and we also gently invite them to wonder further. In addition to the points in the previous sections, then, you might include a couple of questions to potentiate curiosity. For example:

> *We were so excited to see Oliver and Mia work together. It really made us think about what is possible when the children try something new and a little risky. What else might they be able to approach together now that they've done this?*

This communication implicitly acknowledges concerns about risk and safety, while at the same time it invites caregivers to think about what the day's activities mean for their children's broader development. It weaves together your expertise in child development and nature-based education with a nod to their legitimate concerns in a way that is gentle, celebratory, and honest.

It is up to us to show families and caregivers that all of the things children do lead to building competencies in holistic ways. They place immense trust in us, and it is our job as practitioners to hold ourselves accountable to the missions of our program and to show that our philosophy and daily work are meeting children's needs on multiple levels.

Child resting on a log

Response 3. Documenting Children's Experiences in Nature to Invite New Conversations

Our goal in documenting children's experiences in nature must emphasize the nature part. We have to help parents and families not only to see that their child is comfortable at school, but to constantly notice the value of their child's engagement with the natural world. For many families, this value is the core of their desire to be part of our program. To this end, we also consistently link documentation back to children's lived experience. Some examples might include the following:

- focusing on a child's relationship with an element (such as a particular love of water, insects, or mud)
- focusing on our community as a whole (such as noting ways in which children's experiences with the natural world are, simultaneously, part of community connection), exploring how the seasons influence the child as a human rather than how they fit into a particular curriculum (such as noting how falling leaves inspired children to think about cycles of activity and rest rather than describing the day's lesson on hibernating animals), documenting nature-based experiences (such as the everyday beauty of walking barefoot on grass)

Worms held by a child

Documenting children's experiences with nature shows caregivers that we are making good on our commitment to support their children in, and enrich their lives through, interaction with nature. It also helps us as educators to deepen our awareness of, and to build confidence in sharing with outside audiences, the value of nature-based education for children. More than anything, however, observing, documenting, sharing, and deepening our appreciation for children's work honors children's processes of forming connections to nature. Furthermore, we learn to see the subtleties of what true connection to nature looks like. We speak to caregivers not from an authoritative position as educators who know more than they do, but by using the concrete experiences of their children, the humans they love and care for most, as rich and detailed evidence for our claims. We can, in doing this, move beyond our popular imaginative images of children running barefoot through flowers and learn to notice things like cadence and stride length. Who runs? When? How do they run? We can see a child climbing a tree and think not only about the risky play involved or the gross- or fine-motor processes. We can also ask: What does this climbing of a tree indicate about a child's understanding of nature? How might climbing trees help children feel connected to nature and the outdoors?

By asking these sorts of questions, we begin to slowly push the needle of conversation in new directions. We have listened to families' enthusiasm and reservations, showed them that we are supporting their children in the domains in which they display most concern, and demonstrated our capability in speaking to academic outcomes. Seeing families and demonstrating these competencies builds and solidifies trust, and from this foundation of trust we can begin to pose new and different questions to families, to ourselves, and to the world. It all begins with an open mind, an open heart, and a commitment to documenting children's daily lives, work, creativities, and explorations in the great outdoors.

Reflection Questions

1. Think about your current practices of documentation. How are you documenting children's experiences in the outdoors? What experiences do you focus on, and why?
2. What do your families tend to express interest in, or curiosity or concerns about, when it comes to their children's participation in the life of your program? How might you use a piece of documentation to respond to them? To show them the ways that children are building (and already have!) skills and dispositions that will serve them well for many years to come?
3. What sorts of conversations do you wish families, caregivers, and your community were having about children in nature? How and in what ways might your documentation contribute to or help to catalyze these discussions?
4. How can you use your documentation, either process or product, to build a sense of belonging and enthusiasm about children's experiences outdoors in your community?

References

Edwards, Carolyn, Lella Gandini, and George Forman, eds. 2012. *The Hundred Languages of Children: The Reggio Emilia Experience in Transformation.* 3rd ed. Praeger.

Grady, Ron. 2024. *Honoring the Moment in Young Children's Lives: Observation, Documentation, and Reflection.* Redleaf Press.

Paris, Django, and H. Samy Alim, eds. 2007. *Culturally Sustaining Pedagogies: Teaching and Learning for Justice in a Changing World.* Teachers College Press.

Stacey, Susan. 2023. *Pedagogical Documentation in Early Childhood.* 2nd ed. Redleaf Press.

Wurm, Julianne P. 2007. *More Working in the Reggio Way.* Redleaf Press.

CHAPTER 5

Roots and Wings

Vanessa Miot, Atlanta, GA

Vanessa Miot works at Park Pride, a nonprofit organization in Atlanta, Georgia. There she supports neighborhoods that want to activate the power of their parks and green spaces through advocacy. She is also the founder of *Wild Sprout*, a magazine for children ages five to twelve who are curious about the outdoors. Its mission is to encourage environmental education, stewardship, and advocacy through culturally diverse stories presented in a playful, accessible, and empowering way.

There I was, new to the "hood"—motherhood—with no prior experience with children or manual to guide me. Following a period of rest and self-care, I found myself instinctively grabbing the stroller and heading outdoors. What I took for granted, my daughter found captivating, leaving her in awe and tickled by curiosity. Initially, for me, the walks were just a way to keep her busy and to keep me moving, but then I began to go at a slower pace. I chose to spend a little more time with a leaf, pausing to listen to the calls of the birds or to get closer to the ground, leaning in to explore the worlds that exist right under our noses.

Our daily walks rewarded me by revealing subtle but surprising changes in our tropical Miami environment, so that each day became a new adventure of discovery. I was hooked. By the time my daughter was a year old, I had already taken a hard fall down the rabbit hole of nature play, reading everything I could find about its impact on childhood development and how I could best serve as a facilitator. Never mind the thick blanket of humidity of the South Florida summer—I was convinced that I had stumbled across the "cheat sheet" to motherhood somewhere along my route. Nature. And *everyone* needed to know about it.

I grew up outside. My family lived in Florida's Tampa Bay area, and the beach felt like our backyard. Our school was just across the street from the shore, and on weekends my mom and I would spend hours there, watching the gulls and collecting shells to take home and identify. I remember fishing along the pier with my dad, heading home with the windows down, taking in the salt air, and

Mom and me

Sage looks up

listening to Bob Marley, looking forward to eating the day's catch. On other days, I might be enjoying a walk in the park or around the neighborhood with the elders of our family after church. I wasn't new here. But with my child, everything was different.

Every day, multiple times a day, I set out on my trek. I became more familiar with the neighbors, the birds, and the spiders. Months passed and my daughter was more alert, lifting her head and looking about. I would pause to describe the textures of leaves and the distinct smell of the smallest flowers. Words began to form, followed by questions that carried her little feet from one adventure to the next. Life was moving extremely fast, but these walks through our neighborhood seemed to slow everything down as we frequently lowered ourselves to the ground, peering at the insects as they darted around.

Sage looking closer

Staying home with my daughter to nurture this curiosity and explore the world again with her at her pace, I dove into the world of nature play, researching the benefits the natural world has on the development and overall health of children. The internet ushered me toward book titles like *How to Raise a Wild*

Child by Scott D. Sampson and *Last Child in the Woods* by Richard Louv. Both served as incredible resources.

I was thankful for the perspective, but I only heard one voice, the White male voice, in these books—so I kept searching.

My daughter and I soon ventured out in search of programs within our local community. Living in South Florida, we were never short of outdoor activities. The unique habitats served as beautiful spaces to connect and grow both with each other and nature. The park systems readily took advantage of this and offered toddler programs like Nature Tots and Tots on Trails that were designed to foster an awareness of wildlife through environmental-themed independent learning and cooperative play. Nature centers and the playgrounds with the best tree canopies were our haven. Tactile experiences, animal encounters, and events that focused on everything from science to art and making new friends became our weekly rhythm. Enrolling in a forest school would have been ideal, but considering the cost to our modest one-income household, my husband and I thought it best to continue designing our own experience.

Perhaps it was the subject matter, the time of day, or inadequate marketing to a diverse audience, but those in attendance at the nature programs in my area were predominantly White. I seldom encountered families that resembled mine, and I rarely saw representation from other cultural or racial groups. Could the significant distance between neighborhoods predominantly home to Black and Brown families and these experiences be a major barrier for some, especially when factoring in considerations such as nap times, work schedules, and commuting distances? Was this the nature gap at play?

The term *nature gap* refers to the disparity in access to nature and outdoor spaces influenced by race, income, and age. A key issue often raised in discussions about parks and green spaces is the enduring impact of historical redlining. This includes years of disinvestment in affected communities, segregated parks with restricted access for Black residents, environmental and health inequities, and social and economic disparities—all of which continue to exacerbate this divide. The lack of representation in these spaces makes it challenging for individuals to feel connected to nature when they seldom see others who resemble themselves.

I had the luxury of being at home with my child and attending such programs, even though I was piecing it all together on a meager budget. I didn't feel as if I was treated differently at these programs; I felt welcomed, and my child was never excluded. I often met other friendly mothers who would exchange pleasantries. To be honest, I was raised in the suburbs and attended predominantly White schools from third grade until my postgraduate program, so I did not feel uncomfortable. But being a daughter of immigrant parents and having

Exploring

At the nature center

Exploring at home

had the opportunity to be in learning spaces with people from different parts of the world, I couldn't help but think how these programs missed the opportunity to connect us more to the stories of the land and to one another.

It was around this time that I rediscovered a long-forgotten hobby: birding. One of my earliest memories is from when I was about five years old—my mother hung a bird feeder outside the window of my and my sister's bedroom. I remember hearing the soft tapping on the glass from a delighted bird drawn to its breakfast feast. My mother would carefully open the blinds as my sister and I perched eagerly on the edge of the bed, watching in awe as the bright red bird enjoyed its meal.

Life moved on, and I forgot about that red bird at the feeder—until one day on a walk with my daughter, a hawk suddenly swooped down, attacking a bird right above us and showering us with feathers. Not long after, I found myself at Bird Day, hosted by Tropical Audubon, eager to learn more about these amazing creatures. I shared my newfound interest with my mother, who replied, "Oh yes, you were really into birds when you were younger. You even said you wanted to be an ornithologist."

Birds quickly became part of our daily rhythm. Our sit spot on the front steps turned into a place to identify and tally the birds flying overhead. A DSLR camera, gifted by my husband, soon accompanied us on our walks, allowing me to capture memories of these incredible animals—many of whom had traveled thousands of miles only to cross paths with me by chance. Sharing my photographs and "Park Mom" adventures on social media sparked interest from other families. Eventually, becoming weary of traveling across town for nature programs, I decided to start leading family bird walks right in our community. My offerings were warmly received by children and parents alike:

> "Look at what you started! All of them have binoculars now and love bird-watching."

> "My kids are sitting outside . . . enjoying a new level of stillness and curiosity . . . while listening to a woodpecker that they would've never noticed prior to experiencing bird-watching with you! You did this, friend!"

The park adventures continued as my husband and I went on to have two more children and moved to Atlanta, Georgia. I took an audacious leap into a new career field and found joy in working at the crossroads of nonprofit and local government, joining the Park Pride organization. As part of a team committed to parks, I am privileged to support both seasoned and new park advocates who strive to make their voices heard for their parks. My role involves helping them navigate advocacy efforts, particularly in pushing for more resources in areas lacking parks or those historically disinvested—addressing the nature gap. I'm pleased to report that the City of Atlanta recognizes the vital role parks play within its city limits. For example, in the 2025 city budget, there was an increase of $4.1 million (7.9 percent) from the previous year, aimed at enhancing park maintenance to promote safety.

Additionally, through a combination of philanthropic and private funding, organizations like Park Pride have been instrumental in improving my local parks. In 2024 Park Pride awarded $3.9 million for improvements across 37 parks in the City of Atlanta and DeKalb County, with about 50 percent of these funds earmarked for projects in historically disinvested communities. These

Birding together

Sage birding

projects included new playground equipment, pavilions, skate/wheel parks, dog parks, ADA accessibility features, trails, drinking fountains, picnic tables, and more.

It was through my advocacy work that I recognized a gap in the audience I was reaching and began to imagine the impact of sharing this work with children. Through storytelling, we could shift the focus from distant wildlife to the vibrant and diverse ecosystems within our urban spaces. There is a need for stories that not only explore the land and its history but also guide readers through time, showcasing the people—just as diverse as the nature around us—who have shaped our relationship with the environment. By offering bold visions for the future and celebrating the rich ecological diversity of urban neighborhoods, we can inspire local engagement and advocacy to protect and cherish what surrounds us. This realization led me to create *Wild Sprout* magazine—a platform to spark children's curiosity, foster learning, and cultivate stewardship, encouraging a lifelong connection to the natural world.

Across the country, we must address the neglect of parks in underinvested communities if we want nature-based programs to thrive there. Whether it's creating sidewalks, enhancing pedestrian crosswalks, establishing new parks, or maintaining existing ones, the focus must be on ensuring safety and creating inviting spaces for residents. This issue extends systemically.

Sage climbing

Looking down on a bridge

Playing together at the river

In my heart, this is my way of helping that new mother I was six years ago who needed access, options, and opportunity. A parent who was seeing the world again alongside her child and knew that something didn't feel right but wasn't sure what to do next.

As for my daughter and her brothers, my husband and I see to it that their appreciation and curiosity for the natural world are nurtured daily. I provide a thoughtfully chosen collection of books that serve as windows, mirrors, and doors. As a family, we have museum memberships and park passes, and we actively participate in local groups such as 4-H and environmental justice programming led by organizations like the West Atlanta Watershed Alliance. Our unhurried explorations create a brave space for the children to ask questions while I provide the necessary tools for research. I do my best to see that their roots in this practice are strong. I am grateful for a community of educators, scientists, teachers, and park rangers who contribute to giving my children wings.

Family

Emmanuel and Udonis

Sage's garden harvest

Reflection Questions

1. How can early childhood educators use experiences outdoors to foster curiosity, exploration, and language development in young children, regardless of their background or training?

2. Reflecting on the text, how can educators address the disparities in access to nature-based programs and experiences, particularly for families from underrepresented communities, and ensure that all children have equitable opportunities to connect with the natural world?

3. Considering the author's journey from participant to leader in nature-based programs, how can educators collaborate with local communities and governments to advocate for the creation and maintenance of inclusive outdoor spaces that meet the diverse needs of young children and families?

SECTION II

Fostering Community and Cultural Connection Through Nature

I HAVE A PROFOUND sense that nature play in BIPOC communities is different from how it is portrayed in the mainstream media. While play is an integral part of child development, for communities of color the distinction between play and work is not always so clear-cut. In many communities of color, nature play is simply part of everyday living. I can't remember a moment when my parents took me to a particular location to play. I don't have memories of going to a playground, nor do I have memories of going outdoors into a natural area with the specific intent to "play." Yet, my childhood was full of play in nature. I remember helping my *papi* plant crops in our teeny urban backyard plot. I remember making mud with my *primas*, cousins, and picking vivid magenta bougainvillea flowers off bushes to make mud pies in the yard of my *tío*, uncle, in Guatemala. I still hear the sound of the hands of my *abuela*, my grandmother Toya, in the early morning, rhythmically clapping to make *tortillas* by hand as I tried so hard to mimic her movements. In those moments of play, I felt joy. In those moments when I was helping my *papi* and my *abuela*, I also felt useful, an integral part of the work of keeping the household running.

In a study published in 2014 (Alcalá et al.), researchers found that children of families of Indigenous Mayan heritage in Guadalajara, Mexico, contributed voluntarily and meaningfully to the household much more often than did children in middle-income White families in the United States. Researchers noted that these children had more unstructured time to play, with 74 percent of the Indigenous Mayan caregivers reporting that their children had a lot of time for free play, while 43 percent of the non-Indigenous European caregivers reported the same. Yet, these same children of Indigenous heritage, while having more free time to play, also found more time to help around the household. These children helped two times as often and sometimes without even being asked. The Indigenous-heritage children noticed when help was needed and took it upon themselves to help, showing more intrinsic motivation. I was that child, and I believe that my natural inclination to help came about because the "work" I did as a child not only contributed meaningfully and made me feel needed but also felt playful. Taking care of the indoor and outdoor plants, feeding the family dog, and helping my *abuela* make tortillas over the clay hearth all felt joyful. These early experiences instilled in me the value of being helpful and also imprinted nature as a place of joy, as outdoor activities were everywhere and in everything I did as part of my culture. If you were to ask any of the Indigenous-heritage children from the study if they felt they were playing in nature when they fed the chickens or washed the dishes in the *pila*, the large stone sink, they most likely would not describe it that way. But they might agree that the work they did in their household made them feel important, proud, and like they belonged.

The authors in section 2 all find ways to garner the strength of their communities to reconnect children and families not only to nature but to the cultural understandings people of color have in engaging with the natural world. These authors grasp that nature play encompasses everything children do in and with the natural world, simply because the definition of nature play is different for communities of color. Alicia Garcia shares how she uses food to connect to the families she serves and brings to light how engaging with food welcomes communities of color into playing in nature. Pilar Carmina Gonzalez connects culture and nature to create significant moments of learning for children and their families. In many ways, these authors connect the "why" of nature-based learning back to the culture of the families to create a sense of belonging in nature. And finally, Ranita Anderson shares how centering the stories of Black and Brown children in nature-based literature can engage lifelong learning. As you read this section, consider how the perspectives shared by these authors reinforce the idea that nature play is deeply intertwined with cultural identity and community belonging within BIPOC communities.

Reflection Questions

1. According to the author, how does her personal experience as a child challenge traditional notions of "nature play" and blur the lines between work and play? In your experience, do you agree that these lines between work and play are blurred within BIPOC communities?

2. Reflect on a childhood memory of a time when you felt joy and belonging while engaging in an activity that others might perceive as work. How does this memory resonate with the author's experiences?

3. Consider the findings from the study on children of Indigenous Mayan heritage in Guadalajara, Mexico. How do these findings challenge commonly held assumptions about the relationship between play, work, and intrinsic motivation?

References

Alcalá, Lucía, Barbara Rogoff, Rebeca Mejía-Arauz, Andrew D. Coppens, and Amy L. Dexter. 2014. "Children's Initiative in Contributions to Family Work in Indigenous-Heritage and Cosmopolitan Communities in Mexico." *Human Development* 57 (2-3): 96–115. https://doi.org/10.1159/000356763.

CHAPTER 6

The Yummiest Parts of Nature

Alicia Garcia, Deerfield Beach, FL

Alicia Garcia, founder of Project Flourish, is a private chef, designer, and novice urban gardener. In collaboration with her community partners, Alicia offers food literacy programming and a thoughtfully curated collection of provisions with an emphasis on nature, wellness, and sustainability. Alicia holds degrees in both culinary arts and fashion design, as well as certifications in nature-based education and plant-based nutrition. Her hope is that through her offering, learners are inspired to form deeper connections with nature, nourish their bodies and minds, and establish successful rhythms for living—all the best conditions to thrive.

So many beautiful life happenings intertwine with food. Personal celebrations, professional events, seasonal milestones, and cultural experiences alike center around the table. When a new baby arrives or a loved one passes, a family is nourished with meals. Food has long been a love language, an energy exchange, and one of the natural world's greatest gifts.

Like many children, I gained my first bit of independence in the kitchen. My growing ability to prepare food for myself with agency and creativity that yielded delicious results came with a sense of pride. Food was incredibly social in my Caribbean American household. I come from a large Jamaican family, and I was raised in sunny South Florida. So, you could count on the following at any Sunday dinner: reggae music, laughter, good weather, green spaces, fresh fish, and whatever else was currently fruitful from everyone's yards—callaloo, ackee, avocado, cassava, sorrel, plantains, peppers, mangos, and more. The blend of generations gave us a gateway to wisdom, great storytelling, new kitchen skills, and the sharing of old family recipes. From very early on, I learned to love and appreciate the way our meals created community. Not only did I join my family in the kitchen, but I also led my high school cooking club. It wasn't much of a surprise that I found my way to culinary arts school after graduating, or even that I married a fellow chef. However, finding my way to education was truly serendipitous.

My Work and My Why

Running a school lunch catering business for over ten years put me in many different educational spaces. I'd meet with principals and directors, learning about their schools and how they wanted to engage with food on campus, before building out sustainable lunch operations to meet their needs. I observed much and questioned even more. I also assessed the quality of these various programs from a parent's perspective and thought deeply about how learners were responding to their environments. I came to my own conclusions about what really mattered and best served a school family. Outdoor time, green spaces, and the schools' philosophies around food were crucial factors in the temperament of their learners. The class sizes, how well teachers were supported, and how many years students stayed with the same teachers/learning pod mattered more than the fancy tech or curriculum. Whether the program was private or public, it was always about the culture.

I was already teaching seasonal cooking classes for the school communities I catered for throughout Metro Atlanta, but this deep dive into education in June 2016 pivoted my family into homeschooling for our four children. Our babies were eleven, ten, four, and two at the time, so we were taking on middle school, upper elementary, and preschool. Full-time catering was too much of a demand on top of my care for my family, so I took on a new opportunity to manage a historically Black farmers market in Athens, Georgia. This experience planted seeds within myself and my family that are still blooming today. It became crystal clear to me that I could use each week's market and abundant harvest to explore math, science, literature, social studies, and beyond with my children in a tangible way. Not only were we all learning, but the social-emotional benefits of incorporating community, culture, and caretaking were priceless.

Farmers market

Food for thought

We had grace in our day in place of a traditional bell-driven schedule. Our outdoor spaces were equally stimulating as a typical classroom, just in more satisfying ways. Better-quality food and more opportunities for movement brought about better moods, and better moods increased our eagerness to participate. My children's teachers included myself and a collective of community artisans who spoke from their areas of expertise: local farmers, beekeepers, carpenters, bread makers, and small business owners. We were doing everything from taking soil samples to building bat houses for mosquito control, creating signage for market advertisements, managing cash registers, and weighing and packaging produce. My children loved every minute of it. It was real and it made sense beyond the confines of a textbook. Yet when textbooks came into play, that was OK too, because they now had more relevance with these ties to the real world. I knew this approach was something more children needed to experience. I remember telling a dear friend that I wanted to create a learning community around nature-based home economics, one that was interdisciplinary. I wasn't entirely sure what I was doing, but I needed to give myself the permission to do it, and I would call it "Project Flourish" because we were all thriving. My children each had the benefits of self-paced, hands-on learning led by experts from our community that reinforced a sense of purpose, within an ecosystem that looked like them and made their achievements seem attainable. They loved being helpful stewards alongside peers, family, and community members, and they found joy and pride in sharing beautiful foods, set to the backdrop of nature.

Plant Forward for the Win

Fast-forward to 2016. My family was moving back to South Florida. We were exploring new opportunities for school and work, but I was determined to harness the energy from our homeschooling experience with the farmers market. Project Flourish Community officially took shape, with nature-based home economics programming. My offering of classes focused on plant-forward eating, natural apothecary, and seasonal crafting.

I made up my mind that I was committed to teaching "general education" through food literacy and food labs, but I was stumped on how to scale beyond my kitchen-classroom and garden. I wondered if my approach was really applicable for pre-K through twelfth grade. I considered the financial picture, choking hazards, allergies, and levels of compliance associated with traditional brick-and-mortar schools. I realized that green space was the solution to so many of my concerns. Green space gave us a cost-effective classroom, and it was already stocked with a variety of hands-on learning manipulatives and an ever-evolving curriculum for all ages. Children would have freedom of movement as well as a calming place to just *be*. Outside in this wondrous space that serves everyone, we're all guests . . . educators, parents, and children alike. Have you ever thought about what a difference that makes? It creates nuances that adjust the authority just enough for us to interact as curious allies in pursuit of knowledge. I started with summer camps and weekend classes, eventually adding field trips and a yearlong homeschool series.

Growing our own ingredients was another success. Plant-forward recipes are more inclusive of various diets and allergies. There are fewer sanitation liabilities than when working with animal proteins, making it easier to accommodate more learners in a variety of settings. Messes can easily be absorbed into the land, watered away, or perhaps turned into a meal for a forest friend. Making a mess in this environment brings more excitement and curiosity than angst. Nature has a way of doing that—taking a bit of the pressure off. A spill in a classroom has somewhat predictable outcomes: a frustrated teacher, a pause for cleanup, and perhaps a child with big feelings because of the heightened tension. However, outdoors we're already at the will of nature, and messes are common and easily managed. Mistakes become welcomed opportunities. We questioned, "What might grow where we spilled those beans?" We observed insects attracted to certain ingredients, and we documented physical changes caused by the warmth of the sun. More inquiry!

Curating your own food supply can be achieved in many ways: by simply planting seeds in the ground, by creating a container garden if that's all your space

Garden tower harvest

allows for, or by planning a series of raised beds. We started with a tower garden system and sourced whatever else we wanted to eat from the market weekly. Everything tasted better, and everyone noticed! We had children effortlessly eating fresh produce as they harvested it and making comparisons between the bold flavors of garden produce as compared to store-bought counterparts. As one child put it, "Our garden salsa doesn't taste anything like the one from the store. I like tomatoes now!" Veggies became an easy sell at any meal as we happily prioritized farmer friends over big-box grocers.

Harvest

Truly the biggest win for me was the emotional buy-in. Seemingly picky eaters were now eager to set up workstations and explore new recipes. Parents were happy to continue my approach at home, introducing new ingredients with food stories reflective of their culture, practicing math via recipe conversions, and encouraging mud kitchen play in lieu of screen time.

Nature play can be met with apprehension from communities of color. We may not have grown up with it ourselves to have the muscle memory to share with our children. Perhaps we were not allowed to mess up our freshly done hair, or maybe we resided in a heavily populated city with planned playgrounds that dictated how we could use our time outside—or maybe we had no access to playgrounds at all. Whatever the circumstances, food can serve as an easy entry into nature; it's a language of love we speak fluently. We recognize food's value, with its opportunity for fellowship, skill-building ability, and connection to so much more. Through nature-based learning via food play, I was witnessing children of all ages and walks of life willing to forage, climb trees, hold picnics, journal about nature, practice practical math, and embrace mud-covered everything, joyfully.

Nature has so much to say if we settle down enough to listen! Following nature's rhythm by eating our way through the seasons remains my favorite theme for nature play, lending itself to all sorts of seasonal tools, resources, and place-based inquiry. What's growing locally? What climate conditions influence what grows and when? How much sun exposure do our plants need? How are they affected by local wildlife? How does nature allow for a harvest of water-rich watermelon and cucumbers even during blistering hot summer months? How do gourds and root vegetables sustain us through cold winters? Have you observed how waiting for them to roast encourages a stillness and the desire to take in a warm fire or cup of hot tea? Consider what gifts and opportunities nature offers in your area each season.

Playful Pursuits in Wellness, Accessibility, and Stewardship

My garden cookhouse holds my best recipe for play. This space serves as my outdoor classroom and includes picnic tables, green spaces, a few fruit trees, raised beds, and spaces for learning provocations. A typical food-for-thought exploration starts with wellness trivia. We may review nutritional benefits and foodways or play a game of "Who Am I?" to determine which ingredient(s) we'll celebrate that day. We'll exchange stories and opinions and declare an adventurous willingness to reflect again after sampling the day's efforts.

Next, we focus on the accessibility of local ingredients with a series of playful interactions. We may harvest ingredients, create nature journal entries that include plant profiles, and practice best approaches for washing, peeling, slicing, or mindfully tasting our ingredients in raw form.

Lastly, we turn our thoughts to stewardship, as we caretake ingredients into delicious seasonal dishes. This is truly my favorite part. Intentionally featuring recipes with African and Caribbean origins is another beautiful way to honor BIPOC communities. It creates a curriculum through which many students feel a sense of pride, inclusion, and better understanding. It's an opportunity to

Black-eye pea salad

Corn lab

challenge the narrative of soul food being less healthy, as we breathe new life into these recipes with knowledge, modern approaches, and an abundant local harvest. While cutting our okra for a garden stew, we may hear about how a grandma or auntie usually prepares it.

There is also room for agency and collaboration among students, who work together as workstations are set up, flavor preferences are calculated, and plate presentation is conceptualized. Eight out of ten times our little chefs will clear their plates and voluntarily discuss how they will approach the recipe next time. I'm always grateful for the thought of a next time.

The more I have learned about nature play, the more I hear the terms *learning provocations* and *loose parts*. Learning provocations are simply experiences that invite children to play, wonder, and explore. Typically, these experiences come in a visually pleasing space where children can pick up, touch, and engage objects or loose parts associated with a particular learning theme. The magic behind loose parts is the freedom of open-ended play. There are no instructions or ordered steps to follow. Materials can be moved, redesigned, taken apart, and put back together in many ways. Everyone can be successful because the objective is completely individual.

Students sorting ingredients

Loose parts

I wanted to apply this open-ended approach within my food labs. I realized I could treat a curated offering of ingredients as loose parts from which children could build recipes. It's a vibrant and immersive way to get learners curiously engaged. This fun form of inquiry gives children a chance to familiarize themselves with their ingredient options and form their own opinions. Recipe creations are usually very well received by students because all decisions are their own. I've only offered space, materials, and guidance when requested.

A good example is my "I can eat a whole plant" soup challenge. After identifying basic plant anatomy, students sort ingredients into categories: leaves, stems, flowers, and roots. The goal is to build their own soup dish by including selections from each category. My provocation setup features a warm simmering pot of veggie broth, a farmers market–style display of ingredients that can be easily steamed in broth, and food prep workstations. We always end with recipe reflections, when everyone gets an opportunity to share their yummy creations.

Interdisciplinary Nature-Based Food Labs

I always wanted to build a program that grew with my children as they grew. I see so many beautiful learning communities that no longer consider nature play as a priority beyond a certain age or grade. Yet as adults, we're still seeking out nature to soothe and teach us. The COVID-19 pandemic was a great reminder of nature's importance for everyone. So, I want to share some ideas for incorporating nature-based food play well beyond the primary years:

Garden Demo

- **Food for thought within mathematics:** arithmetic for recipe conversion, food fractions, veggie symmetry, measurements of liquids versus solids, food costs with percentages, food taxation, economics, supply/demand in respect to climate change or natural disasters
- **Food for thought within science:** botany, permaculture, agriculture, food sciences, natural apothecary, sustainability, and environmental science
- **Food for thought within social studies:** hunters and gatherers' eating habits and culinary practices, food trade, food history, cultural cuisines, food geography, recipe origin stories, kitchen tools and artifacts, legislation (including food labels, government-funded nutrition programs, and agricultural practices)
- **Food for thought within English/language arts:** food stories, food or nature poetry slams, writing prompts, documenting the properties of plants, natural world or culinary vocabulary, scavenger hunts

All these ideas can be combined with plant-forward food labs to keep nature at the focus of learning for years to come.

My Reflections

I'm rooting for all children and especially advocating for our beautiful Black and Brown babies. Project Flourish Community has been my vessel. I live in South Florida where the educational disparities are wide, despite how wonderfully diverse our population is. I could go on and on about state politics, banned books, and economic strife. Instead, I've chosen to simply lean into this resourceful landscape (with its robust community and natural resources alike) to seek solutions with the same ingenuity my ancestors always did. South Florida has much to offer in terms of nature-based education, and my hope is to see it continue to grow. Our weather allows for year-round learning explorations with unique opportunities within agriculture, heavily influenced by our global community.

Junior chefs

Making nature discoveries via food play answers the call for me. It's purposeful work that serves others and in turn serves me. A sense of joy, pride, and safety reaches each of my students. That's the priority since learning can't effectively happen without those conditions being achieved first. Once they are, we can tackle bigger topics. We get to touch on the wellness that nature provides in a fun and tangible way. We talk about combating health conditions like diabetes, which are so prevalent within our community, and we work to make shifts in our diet that can make all the difference in our health. We discuss food sovereignty and apprenticeship with food-service industries, and we build life skills that lay the foundation for economic mobility throughout high school and beyond. We celebrate our rich history, beginning well before slavery, and sample a myriad of cuisines that have derived from the movement of peoples.

Wherever we gather to break bread, I quietly consider it a liberation table. There is agency in every part of our play, from setting up our workstations just so to harvesting ingredients that speak to us, crafting unique recipes, and finally sharing our talents with our loving community. These gifts are a lifetime investment in self, thanks to the generosity of nature.

Reflection Questions

1. What ingredients and foodways in your area celebrate local lands and communities of color? How can you incorporate them into your nature studies?
2. How can educators infuse cultural significance and inclusion into food-based experiences in your community?
3. In what ways can you invite families to share their cultural practices around food and make them part of the culture of your classroom and school (for example, potlucks, heritage month celebrations, ingredients spotlights)?
4. What types of cooking experiences can you accommodate? For example, can you cook hot meals, or do you need to start with raw recipes? What equipment or infrastructure might you gradually add to improve your cooking experiences?

CHAPTER 7

Incorporating Language and Cultural Learning into Nature-Based Early Childhood Programs

Pilar Carmina Gonzalez, Los Angeles, CA

Pilar Gonzalez is the cofounder and director of Aventuras Forest School in Los Angeles, CA. Before starting Aventuras, she spent seven years as an education researcher at EDC, focusing on education technology and early childhood education, including creating resources for preschool teachers in collaboration with leading experts in dual-language learning. Pilar previously taught reading, writing, and English as a Second Language for five years in grades K–4 in New York City.

She holds a bachelor's degree in history and science from Harvard, a master's degree in sociology and education from Columbia University Teachers College, and a master's in teaching English to Speakers of Other Languages. She has also studied early childhood education at UCLA Extension and is a certified Cedarsong Way Forest Kindergarten and Kidding Around Yoga children's yoga teacher.

When we moved from New York City to Los Angeles in 2017, my husband, Roberto, and I couldn't find a preschool for our son, Adrian, that had everything we felt was important for his physical, emotional, and cultural development. So, in 2018 we started our own preschool! Aventuras is now one of only a handful of preschools in the United States to combine language immersion with a fully outdoor setting.

The traditional forest school model appealed to us because it encourages social-emotional and environmental learning that flows from the children's daily experiences. And since maintaining Adrian's heritage language was important to us, we added Spanish language immersion. But as time went on, we began to feel that something else was missing from this model. Our family, and the families that our school attracted, felt passionate about teaching our children how to be responsible, empathetic citizens of the world, so we decided to add social and cultural topics to our curriculum. In this chapter, we'll tell the story in more detail of why we founded the school and how we make sure that language, culture, and social change are every bit as much a part of our curriculum as nature, environmental awareness, and social-emotional development.

My Background in Nature, Language, and Biculturalism

My interest in nature and my bicultural identity had their roots in my early childhood in Argentina, with an Argentine dad and American mom. My mom was an English and science teacher, and I have vivid memories of doing science

Aventuras Forest School was founded as a fully outdoor Spanish immersion preschool in 2018, set primarily in Griffith Park, a large urban park in Los Angeles. We have twelve students aged three to six and three teachers, including myself. I act as the cofounder, director, and lead teacher, and we employ two other teachers. We also run a small Parent & Me program in the afternoons for two-year-olds. Our school was inspired by forest school traditions such as those espoused by Cedarsong, one of the oldest forest schools in the country, some elements of Waldorf education, and our own philosophy drawn from my years of experience as an educator, researcher, and mother. Our philosophy revolves around three core principles: Taking Care of Ourselves, Taking Care of Each Other, and Taking Care of the Earth. Our flexible curriculum and our everyday practices emphasize feelings, kindness, empathy, community service, multiculturalism, civic engagement, and environmentalism. While most of our day consists of free play, we do come together for some structured activities, including circle time with a gratitude practice and multicultural songs in Spanish; story time with a mix of ABC books, math books, cultural books, and nature books in Spanish; art time with an emphasis on open-ended creativity and independence; and occasional yoga, meditation, and mindfulness. Our program is conducted largely in Spanish, although we rely on English when necessary for communicating with new children who have not yet learned Spanish, for conflict resolution, and for safety reasons. The children are free to communicate with one another in their language of choice.

experiments at home with her. We also made regular visits to a small cabin in northern Patagonia in the middle of a spectacularly beautiful forest.

Although my mom is a native English speaker and taught English at a British school in Buenos Aires, I grew up amid my dad's loving extended family, none of whom spoke a word of English, including my dad. My mom made a valiant effort to teach me English. But by the time I was almost seven and we moved to Providence, Rhode Island, where my American grandparents lived, I had only picked up a handful of English words, and I was quite overwhelmed to be immersed in a new language. In my English as a Second Language classroom, I felt lost and segregated from the other "normal" children in my grade and found myself treated differently as an immigrant. Fortunately, since we lived with my American grandparents who spoke only English, I picked up the new language quickly. My parents were also careful to maintain our cultural ties to Argentina, including frequent trips there, and it became a point of pride for me. I endeavored to maintain my spoken Spanish with my dad, at first out of necessity but then more intentionally as he became fluent in English.

My experiences as a child with bilingualism and biculturalism made me curious about language development and learning, and as an adult I got a master's degree in Teaching English to Speakers of Other Languages. Working with elementary-aged children and families in deeply diverse immigrant communities in New York City was rewarding. But I didn't believe in the traditional educational system, which I found to be quite stifling. There was too much emphasis on testing and on literacy and math to the exclusion of all other subjects. I found that the children I taught hadn't received any kind of social-emotional teaching, which hurt their learning because they were too distracted by their feelings and social conflicts, and as a teacher I was not supported in helping them in those areas. At one school where I taught, a teacher could even get in trouble for teaching arts and crafts to young children because it was not "rigorous" enough. Administrators expected children to be sitting in their seats, focused quietly on their work. But I knew that young children learn best when their bodies are active, when they can talk and sing and interact and play with each other and express themselves through the arts. I decided to quit teaching and pursue a career in education research and policy, with a desire to influence the field of education at a more systemic level.

How Aventuras Got Started

In 2017 Roberto and I moved from New York to Los Angeles; the year-round access to the outdoors was irresistible to us, as two nature lovers with an active and curious two-year-old. We knew what we wanted for Adrian: Spanish-language immersion and plenty of physical activity and outdoors time. Roberto toured a number of preschools in northeast Los Angeles and found that there were surprisingly few programs that incorporated languages. If they did, the typical extent of it was having a Spanish-speaking teacher who sang a few songs a week with the children, rather than a purposeful use of the language in daily routines. He also found the physical facilities lacking. The preschools often had only a small asphalt lot for the children to play.

We discovered a few forest schools and researched the origins of that movement. While the idea of a completely outdoor education was exciting for us, the schools we looked into did not incorporate any languages other than English. After a frustrating day of preschool hunting, my husband asked, "Have you thought about starting your own school? Is that crazy?" To his surprise, I replied, "Yes, I have!"

Child exploring nature, one tree at a time

I had recently come to the realization that starting my own program for preschool-aged children could give me the freedom to implement everything I knew and believed about how young children learn best. At the time, I was working remotely as an education researcher for the nonprofit I had been with for almost eight years. Although I enjoyed the work, having my son made me miss working more directly with children, as I did when I had been a public school elementary English as a Second Language teacher for five years.

I saw how Adrian's own language development was affected by our efforts to teach him Spanish. We started with the "one parent, one language" approach, with my husband speaking Spanish and myself speaking English. We also placed him in home-based child care with a Spanish-speaking family to help promote his Spanish development. However, when we switched to an English-language nanny share when he was around age two, we found that he had become quite English-dominant.

I changed the language I spoke with him to exclusively Spanish and experimented with other ways to enhance his Spanish learning. I read books in Spanish that were rich in vocabulary and illustrations, and we had long conversations about what we saw in the pictures. If he spoke to me in English, I would translate what he said back into Spanish, and he naturally started repeating what I said in Spanish, supplementing his verbal vocabulary and grammar. We sang lots of songs in Spanish together, and when we streamed movies, we set the default language to Spanish. We asked our extended family members, all of whom spoke Spanish, to speak only Spanish to him and in front of him. By the age of three, he was fully bilingual, and of course we did not want to lose all that progress by sending him to an English-only preschool setting.

When we decided to open our school, I participated in an intensive in-person training at another more established forest school, and I also attended a nature-based early education conference, where I gathered ideas about how to design our program. We started out with a very open structure, similar to other forest school programs. We did not have a set schedule or any preplanned activities. However, I felt that we were missing some sort of rhythm or set of routines to shape our day. I sensed also that we were missing an awareness of the larger culture and society that we couldn't provide with a strictly forest school approach, and when the protests surrounding George Floyd's killing by police appeared on the news in the summer of 2020, they only strengthened this sentiment. So, when I attended a training with a Danish Waldorf forest school administrator who mentioned the idea of "breathing in" to come together as a group for an organized activity, and then "breathing out" to give the children the freedom to guide their own learning, the idea immediately resonated with me. This gave us the structure to add some preplanned but flexible activities to the more unstructured free play in nature typical of most forest schools. We added more and more social and cultural exploration to our practices over the years, and these were also a natural fit with our language immersion approach.

What Our Practice Looks Like Today

Ultimately, language and culture are all about human connection. We have found that a great first place to start with incorporating language and culture into educational programs is with the cultures and languages of the staff, enrolled families, and surrounding community. This approach makes even more sense in outdoor programs like Aventuras, which typically value learning from experiences rather than from worksheets and other methods perceived as academic. We have found that since our program emphasizes languages and cultures, it tends to draw families with heritage from diverse cultures, including throughout the Spanish-speaking world: Mexico, El Salvador, Argentina, Colombia, Costa Rica, and Spain.

But we also tend to attract families who have other heritage languages, since multilingual families often value language learning in general, and they see Spanish as a practical language for their children to learn in addition to other languages they are exposed to through their family. Indeed, those children often learn Spanish faster than English-only children, since their brains are already primed for language learning, and those skills easily transfer to different languages. We've had parents who are first- or second-generation immigrants from Singapore, the Philippines, China, South Korea, India, Israel, Kenya, Czech Republic, Hungary, and Italy, among other countries. We also draw from the cultures of the children's nannies and babysitters, who often feel like part of the family; due to the language focus of our school, they often speak Spanish as well. For example, we have had nannies visit our program to share foods from their culture, teach children to make tortillas, and even do our makeup for Día de los Muertos! Finally, we supplement our roster of visitors with members of the community, such as a Mexican American farmer who works with sustainable practices and an expert on the edible plants of Southern California and the traditional foods of American Indian groups in the region, such as the Tongva and Chumash peoples. For visitors from outside the immediate school community, we offer compensation for their time, unless they contacted us first primarily to conduct a school observation.

When we invite visitors to share about their culture, we generally leave it very open-ended so they can share whatever they'd like. Sharing of food is always encouraged since it opens up the children's palates, and it's fun! We also encourage visitors to share in any of the following ways: music, dance, art project, book or story, show-and-tell with cultural objects, or any hands-on activity. Sharing generally takes place when we would normally do morning snack and circle time, or after lunch, with story time followed by art. Below are some examples of some of our most memorable cultural sharing experiences.

One mother of a recent graduate was an elementary Mandarin teacher who had put her teaching days on hold after the birth of her daughter. She always had wonderful ideas for hands-on experiences for the children. One day she brought silk moths the children could hold, which was a great way to combine nature education and cultural education, since silk moths are considered very important in Chinese culture. We were all amazed by these beautiful and otherworldly creatures. They were a ghostly pale white in color and quite large. They were also fuzzy in texture, with very furry antennae. This made for an intriguing sensory experience, using our tactile sense, which is too often neglected in traditional learning. The fuzziness was so intense that some of the children got a bit flummoxed by it! The moths had quite a strong grip on our fingers, and they seemed more like little animals than insects. The experience was unforgettable, and I'll certainly never look at a silk garment the same way again!

Another memorable experience with the same mom was a Chinese calligraphy demonstration. What made it unique was that she brought authentic tools and taught us the traditional method of grinding a dry ink stick against a rock and mixing that powder with water, then using a brush with bristles made of animal hair to make the strokes. What I loved about this experience was being able to pass along ancient practical and cultural knowledge, which makes us

Children holding a silk moth

Child exploring their Chinese calligraphy skills

feel more connected to our ancestors and fits really well into the typical forest school philosophy. Although I was mostly expecting the children to make abstract paintings with the ink and brushes, they were so curious about the calligraphy that they asked the mom to demonstrate how to make the numbers from one to ten in Chinese characters, and many of them copied her. One lunar new year she also told the legend of the animal race that created the Chinese zodiac and illustrated it with puppets she made out of paper. The children loved recreating the race with the puppets afterward!

Oral storytelling of legends and folktales, with or without puppets, is a wonderful tool for sharing culture. As a bonus, legends and folktales usually make nature connections, so they are a great fit for outdoor programs. One example we enjoyed is the book *Coyote Places the Stars*, which explains how constellations were created according to oral tradition from the Wasco people.

Part of what makes these experiences stand out is the way they engage multiple senses, which is great for memory recall. Plus, it makes the learning more fun and engaging. Another way to involve multiple senses in cultural sharing is song and dance. One of our Mexican American teachers was a former Ballet Folklórico instructor. One day she brought in full regalia, including a very wide, long, and colorful skirt made with seemingly endless fabric. She also wore traditional shoes with nails embedded in them to make noise similar to tap-dancing shoes. She let us look at these items up close and feel the texture

Children recreating stories with puppets

of the embroidered fabric and the bottoms of the shoes. Then we played some typical music, and she danced for us on a wooden bridge, which made a very loud sound when she stomped on it with the nails in her shoes! Finally, we imitated her dance moves ourselves, which added another sensory component. Everyone had huge smiles on their faces!

Music and dance are also wonderful ways to support a feeling of connectedness and community. One of our children had a little sister who had just turned one year old. Their father was from a small village in Kenya, and they had recently traveled there for a first-haircutting ceremony and wanted to share the experience with the class. The dad, our student, her big brother, and her baby sister all came to visit. They placed the baby on a stool and had us all dance around her in a circle and pretend to take one snip of her hair. At one point in the ceremony, we all sang each person's name and told them in Kisii, the father's home language, "You are the light!" It was a magical feeling of connection and made each one of us feel very special and appreciated by the group.

Outdoor educators often turn most readily to American Indian and Indigenous knowledge and traditions when looking for cultural inspiration, with good reason. It fits well with forest school ideals to teach children to take care of the land and connect with the ways of our ancestors. However, we have found a few pitfalls with teaching about American Indian/Indigenous cultures in school settings. Without proper research and consultation with people from those communities, it's easy to make mistakes, such as incorrect generalizations like "American Indians lived in tepees," calling their regalia "costumes," referring to them only in the past tense, or perpetuating other inaccuracies or offenses due to a lack of knowledge. This is why we rely on American Indian educators like Abe Sanchez from the Chia Café Collective and books written by American Indian authors to educate both the teachers and the children. We have discovered many wonderful resources over the years, with new ones coming out all the time. We especially love books that are bilingual or trilingual and feature American Indian languages like Cherokee or Nahuatl, such as *Agua, agüita / Water, Little Water*, which includes Spanish, English, and Nahuatl versions of the text. Please consider this only a starting point, and we encourage you to connect with your local community if you'd like to immerse yourself and the children you serve in Indigenous knowledge and practices.

Some of our readings about Indigenous cultures have inspired visual art projects, which are another great multisensory way to combine culture and preschool education. Rather than recreating generic Indigenous objects such as totem poles and tepees out of context culturally, we look for culturally specific crafts drawn from books by American Indian authors. For example, the book *Otsoliheliga / We Are Grateful* written by Traci Sorell, a member of the Cherokee Nation, depicts Cherokee corn husk dolls, which we recreated with the children at school.

Child showing corn husk doll

We find that learning about American Indian foraging traditions and ethnobotany is a great way to help children understand where their food comes from, which reinforces our connectedness to the earth and our need to take care of it. It also helps us connect to the ways our ancestors around the world lived. We originally became interested in the topic through our frequent field trip visits to the nearby Autry Museum of the American West, which is a wonderful resource for information about American Indian cultures and history. One exhibit is about Western American Indian groups and their relationships with the land in topic areas like fire, salmon, and plants. They also have an ethnobotany garden featuring local plants labeled with their traditional uses. It's there that we first learned about the Chia Café Collective, a group of educators and advocates who are knowledgeable about native plants, foraging, and traditional American Indian foods in the areas surrounding Southern California. The collective is interested in the nutritional value of traditional foods such as acorn bread, and it has even published a cookbook, *Cooking the Native Way*, to share recipes and information about these foods.

Child exploring the neighborhood

We've had wonderful hands-on experiences with Abe Sanchez, a founding member of the collective, and invite him to visit once during Native American Heritage Month (November), and once in the spring when different plants are visible. Every visit, Abe leads an engaging activity for the children, such as making tortillas by hand and dyeing them with plant-based dyes, processing acorns into flour, foraging for edible plants to cook into an omelet, and hand pressing prickly pear juice, a fruit called *tuna* in Spanish. He also takes us on a nature walk and always includes background information on native versus invasive plants, teaching how we can live in better harmony with the earth. The children absolutely adore him, and we always write him thank-you letters (dictated by the children) about our great experiences and things we learned.

Abe engaging the children during his visits

Teaching Languages Outdoors

Aside from traditions such as holidays, foods, and folktales, learning a language is a key way that people bridge different cultures. The United States is an outlier in the global community because so many of our people speak only one language; in much of the world, knowing two or even three languages is the norm. We have experienced firsthand how empathy and friendship can blossom when we make an effort to explore the languages of others. While teachers who are not proficient in another language may feel daunted by the prospect of teaching languages to children, they can always find ways to do so in an accessible and engaging way. Songs are a fun, easy, and very effective way to learn languages. It's often easier to pronounce and remember foreign words in song form, especially if they also include fingerplay or body movement, as do songs such as *"Diez deditos"* or *"Juanito cuando baila."* One resource for play rhymes and action songs in Spanish is José-Luis Orozco, a Mexican musical artist who is inspired by traditional Mexican folk music and songs and publishes songs in book form.

Another daily part of our routine for teaching Spanish is storybook time, which often also has a nature connection. We usually start with an introduction in English to help the children comprehend the book more easily. The pictures in books can also provide visual support to help children understand what we are reading. Reading books in another language is a great option for parents or educators who speak a bit of another language but aren't completely confident in their vocabulary and grammar. Sometimes we even read books that were written in English and translate them into Spanish on the fly, using the pictures as visual support. Although some of our stories are Spanish translations of English-language books, we prefer to select books originally written in Spanish or bilingually, especially if they have culturally relevant content, such as biographies of notable people in history or stories of holiday traditions

Scan this QR code or go to www.redleafpress.org/son/7.1.pdf.

in the Spanish-speaking world. We offer a list of recommended books via QR code, and you can consult the foreign language sections of your local library or bookstore for more ideas. If you live in an area with a large Hispanic population, there may even be a Spanish-language bookstore in your community.

We also teach Spanish organically in our everyday conversation using numbers, common Spanish nature words, and words that relate to our daily routines, such as *manos* for hands and *mochilas* for backpacks. Anyone can learn a few simple words like these in any language.

When we think of language education, we also include sign language. One year we had a child with a Deaf grandmother who used to teach elementary school and college, and she led an activity showing the children pictures of nature words and teaching us fun signs like "tiger" in an animated way. Learning a few signs is also very accessible for any educator.

If you or another staff member is fluent in another language, you may be interested in a more immersive approach. In addition to the practices described above, we aim to speak to the children in Spanish about 90 percent of the time, asking them open-ended questions and translating their responses back into Spanish if they answer in English. Of course, we try to be sensitive and keep language learning fun rather than strictly enforcing any rules about what languages children can speak. At this young age, helping them feel supported is most important, so we still use English if they are completely new to Spanish or if there is a safety or social-emotional issue that's too complex to address in their nondominant language. The best resource we've found for parents or educators who want to learn more about raising bilingual children is the book *The Bilingual Edge: Why, When, and How to Teach Your Child a Second Language* by Kendall King and Alison Mackey (Harper Perennial, 2007), which has lots of great tips as well as useful background information in an accessible format.

Tips and Ideas to Use in Nature-Based Programs

There are so many fun and engaging ways to incorporate languages and cultures into outdoor programs! Here is a menu of tips and ideas gleaned from our stories and experiences that you can try in your program:

- Share cultural celebrations, food, music, show-and-tell, and storytelling led by staff, families, or guests from diverse cultures. Recognize the languages and cultural knowledge of staff and families and bring them into the program.
- Invite guests from your local community who have firsthand experiences with diverse languages and cultures to share their knowledge. We encourage you to compensate them for their time and reinforce the learning with cultural context so it's not just a stand-alone, token experience.

- Share folktales from diverse cultures, either directly from books or by retelling orally; these will most likely include nature connections you can discuss. Heighten the experience by using puppets, especially homemade ones.
- Use simple songs and poems in other languages, especially ones with fingerplays, during walks or other shared moments.
- Practice sign language, especially with nature words that will relate to the school environment.
- Learn to count in other languages, which can be done in the context of nature exploration and play.
- Learn simple games and dances from other cultures.
- Learn about specific cultural practices around plants, including preparation of edible plants, medicinal uses of plants, and basket weaving. However, please do your homework about toxic plants in your area and only eat foraged foods that you are completely confident are safe. We do not recommend foraging for mushrooms with children, since even experts can make mistakes.
- Take field trips to museums or other community resources with cultural content (for example, the Autry Museum of the American West).
- Use the target language for words that are often repeated, such as nature words and routine words (*ardilla*/squirrel, *mochila*/backpack).
- Ask open-ended questions in the target language; translate what the children say into the target language.
- When incorporating languages and cultures that are not your own, do thorough research, preferably in consultation with members of that culture, to make sure you are acting with sensitivity and respect.

Although not frequently seen together, cultural and language education can be valuable and easy to include in outdoor early education. We advocate for the inclusion of these subjects to help raise the next generation of responsible and empathetic global citizens. Programs can begin the process by exploring the cultures of their staff, children and families, and larger community, and supplement with books, songs, and folktales from diverse cultures. Cultural holidays and foods are other accessible entry points. Studying the plant-based foods and foraging practices of local Indigenous groups is a great way to bridge culture and nature. You can even explore other languages with the children to varying degrees depending on your own knowledge of that language. When in doubt, be sure to consult with sources who come from the community you are sharing with the children, compensating them for their time and efforts as appropriate. And above all, have fun!

Reflection Questions

1. How do the cultures and languages represented by your staff, children, families, and the broader community shape the values and experiences in your school or organization?
2. What cultural institutions in your community could you visit with the children? How might these visits enhance their appreciation for different cultures? In what way can you bring this understanding to the children's families?
3. Which community members could you invite to share their cultural experiences with the children, and how might their stories enrich the children's understanding of diversity?
4. Which holidays are celebrated within your target cultures, and how can exploring these traditions deepen the children's understanding of cultural diversity?
5. What are some simple songs and folktales from the target cultures that you could use with the children?
6. What cultural months, such as Asian American/Pacific Islander Heritage Month, could you explore with the children?
7. Who might you consult, or what resources from the target community could you leverage, to ensure that what you share with the children is accurate, thoroughly researched, and culturally respectful?
8. Think about the cultural backgrounds of your school's management and teaching staff. What gaps in knowledge, blind spots, or implicit biases might exist in the cultural backgrounds of the school management and teaching staff that affect teaching and learning? How can these biases be acknowledged constructively to foster improvement? How can difficult conversations be structured thoughtfully? How can staff address these biases without burdening any cultural group, such as by hiring a diversity, equity, and inclusion consultant rather than asking community members for free advice?

CHAPTER 8

Nature, Literature, and Representation

Ranita Anderson Dawkins, Durham, NC

Ranita, a speech-language pathologist, specializes in supporting families of autistic children and others with developmental needs in communication and language. Passionate about literacy development, she advocates for diverse representation in children's literature. An avid outdoor enthusiast, Ranita enjoys camping, hiking, climbing, and biking, exploring everything from national parks to her own backyard. She combines her love for nature with her expertise in child development to inspire the next generation of environmental leaders and ensure that individuals of all abilities can experience the outdoors. She aims to create a nature/forest school that fosters multigenerational learning and centers diverse perspectives.

Young people, I want to beg of you, always keep your eyes open to what Mother Nature has to teach you. By so doing, you will learn many valuable things every day of your life.
—George Washington Carver

NATURE, WITH ITS rich sensory experiences and dynamic environments, serves as a powerful classroom. This chapter explores the ways in which exposure to and engagement with nature, alongside the centering of diverse children's books and open-ended play, contribute to language and literacy development. From fostering curiosity and creativity to building resilience and problem-solving abilities, outdoor learning plays a multifaceted role in shaping the foundational skills that form the bedrock of lifelong learning.

I am the founder of Rooted in Color. As a speech-language pathologist and someone who has found the peace and joy that nature can bring, I developed this organization to support children and their families to connect and learn in nature, with a specific focus on building language skills. At Rooted in Color, our mission is to foster a deep connection between children, their families, and the natural world through language and literacy. We use diverse picture books as a gateway to begin our exploration and connect the content to immersive nature-based experiences. We cultivate a love for reading and writing, create children's connections with others and the environment, and instill a lifelong

Rooted in Color is focused on providing nature-based speech therapy, literacy programs, camps, and curriculum that center on diverse, inclusive experiences and cater particularly to children, including those from Black and historically underrepresented communities and those with different abilities, including autistic children. Through therapeutic and educational activities, we combine outdoor experiences with culturally relevant, diverse children's books to create spaces where children connect meaningfully with nature, develop language skills, and feel represented. Additionally, we work to support families in ensuring they can engage their children in similar learning opportunities outside of our programming. We collaborate with local schools, organizations, and conservation partners to create programming that aligns with environmental stewardship while fostering language and literacy skills.

appreciation for the environment. Through innovative programs, engaging activities, and community partnerships, we empower young learners to become compassionate and articulate communicators who are inspired to protect and preserve our planet while enhancing their academic skills.

Nature and Literacy

Nature provides endless opportunities for curiosity and exploration. This happens, for example, as children observe plants, see how animals move, or discover what floats or sinks in a pond or puddle. Through these observations, children can develop hypotheses, a foundational skill in learning. As children continue to grow in the complexities of their learning, natural spaces offer unpredictable challenges, encouraging individuals to engage in critical thinking and problem-solving. Negotiating natural obstacles, identifying patterns, and adapting to changing environments all help build cognitive flexibility and analytical skills. One of the key elements in all of this is play.

Although many think of nature as a remote location with vast amounts of trees and maybe even a body of water, when we think about nature for the purpose of this chapter, we are considering any accessible outdoor space that offers the opportunity to move and learn. This could be a backyard, a playground, the courtyard of an apartment complex, or a city, county, or state park. While different in the opportunities they offer, the list of nature places is endless, and so are the chances to gather new knowledge, when we ensure that the outdoor play spaces are inclusive and welcoming to children from diverse backgrounds. We can do this by incorporating elements that reflect the cultural diversity of the community, making the outdoor environment a space where everyone feels represented and valued. By integrating diverse books into nature-based activities, educators can create a holistic learning experience that fosters a love for literature, a drive to explore nature, and an appreciation for diversity among children.

Books are one easy way for children and caregivers to learn about different cultures and experiences. This exposure allows readers to understand others and embrace experiences that they otherwise might not pursue. Similarly, reading takes families to new places. Lyrics from the theme song of the classic children's television show *Reading Rainbow* highlights this journey: "I can go anywhere." "Anywhere" can mean opening a book about a snowy landscape when you are surrounded by beaches, imagining a national park thousands of miles away, or reading about a kayaking trip despite your own inexperience with water and boating. This ability to visit new worlds supports the idea that reading and books engage the imagination.

While books and reading support learning and build connections, we need not just any book, but specifically diverse books. While many strides have been made to support diversity in children's literature, for years we have seen the lack of representation in what is published for children. As recently as 2018, the Cooperative Children's Book Center noted that children's books depict White (50 percent) and animal (27 percent) characters at greater rates than any other group (Stechyson 2019). The proportion of books by BIPOC authors and about BIPOC characters continues to tick up, but more resources are needed. Below we explore the significance of this discrepancy.

Diverse children's books play a crucial role in promoting inclusivity, fostering empathy, and providing representation for children from various backgrounds.

When characters from diverse backgrounds are portrayed in children's books, children see themselves reflected in literature. Representation fosters a sense of belonging and validates the experiences of individuals from underrepresented groups. Providing representative children's books that depict recreation and exploration in nature is essential. Often when we think about diverse books, we think about historically focused books that depict characters struggling through difficult experiences that have shaped the present for many from underrepresented backgrounds. While this narrative can be important, it is also necessary to share everyday experiences and promote simple activities that include people from different backgrounds. For example, fishing is a tradition and skill for many Black and Brown families that has been passed down for generations, but it is difficult to find a picture book that displays this representation. *Daddy and Me, Side by Side* by Pierce Freelon is an excellent representation of a Black father and son engaged in fishing and other outdoor recreation activities. This story promotes the regular experiences of Black families while also providing rich language to support learning.

While each child deserves representative books, it is essential for all people to have exposure to diverse perspectives in children's literature to promote cultural awareness and understanding. Diverse books break down stereotypes, reduce prejudice, and encourage an appreciation for the richness of different cultures. It is important not only for Black and Brown people to see themselves, but for others to recognize and know that there are Black and Brown anglers, kayakers, climbers, rangers, birders, and beyond. This exposure starts in childhood and can be explored in children's literature.

Additionally, hearing diverse stories enhances cognitive development by exposing children to a variety of language styles, vocabulary, and narrative structures. Language and literacy form the cornerstone of cognitive development in children, laying the foundation for effective communication and lifelong learning. Nature, with its diverse sensory stimuli and dynamic settings, presents a rich tapestry for language and literacy development.

Developing language involves acquiring skills in several different categories. These include the ability to understand written or spoken language input (receptive language), the ability to use language to share thoughts and feelings (expressive language), and the ability to communicate in social situations (pragmatic language). Engaging in nature play allows children to practice all these areas of language. Often we are working on all of these areas within a single activity. Educators can also intentionally outline language development goals and integrate these into nature activities. The process of attaching language skills to nature connects these experiences to joy, and weaving practice into everyday occurrences allows children to better retain and apply their skills.

Vocabulary is a key area where books and nature collide. Nature provides an abundance of stimuli, introducing children to a vast array of words associated with tangible items, recreational experiences, and natural phenomena. Exposure to this contextual vocabulary in outdoor settings enhances children's understanding and retention of words. Books that center nature-based themes often include vocabulary that is unique to these experiences. Highlighting this vocabulary in a multimodal way, using all five senses and attaching this information to experiences, is key for children's ability to learn and apply this new language. Another step to further enhance learning is to connect novel language with visuals and synonyms, allowing students to make connections between familiar information and new learning. Adding intentional language learning with the use of diverse children's books offers a structured way to enhance children's expressive language skills. Additionally, expressive language increases as children observe their surroundings and describe what they see.

Nature-based play activities, such as creating stories with found objects or designing outdoor signs, can integrate literacy into play. These types of activities enhance letter recognition, phonemic awareness, and overall literacy skills in an enjoyable and natural way. Group activities in nature, such as nature walks or collaborative projects, provide opportunities for using language socially. Children engage in conversations, express their observations, and articulate their thoughts, contributing to the development of strong pragmatic skills.

We must also consider writing and text when discussing literacy. Nature is filled with environmental print, from signs on trails to labels on plants to maps. Interacting with this print in a real-world context promotes functional literacy, connecting written language to practical applications.

Below, we will explore how these literacy topics all come together. We will use fiction and nonfiction books, engage experiential learning, and support language acquisition through play and application.

In the book *Jayden's Impossible Garden* by Mélina Mangal, recycling and decorating are integral themes. In the story, Jayden shares about an encounter in the neighborhood and why he believes he should be able to build a garden in an urban space with his neighbor. His example supports storytelling and allows children to see and imitate how to relay information and develop an argument. Specific vocabulary in the book centers on flowers: *zinnia, marigold, nasturtium.* These words may be novel to the average child, and their introduction can begin discussion around natural diversity. We highlight important and unique language before, during, and after readings. Experiences and discussions as noted below build on the information from our diverse readings.

When considering nonfiction, *Farmer Will and the Growing Table* by Jacqueline Briggs Martin demonstrates themes of community and perseverance.

The story follows farmer Will Allen as he transforms abandoned urban spaces into gardens to provide fresh food for his community. His story demonstrates resilience and illustrates how one person can inspire change through hard work and dedication. Vocabulary around gardening, such as *compost*, *seedlings*, and *urban farm*, introduces children to concepts of sustainability and food systems. These terms are highlighted to spark discussions about community impact and environmental stewardship. Building on readings like these, hands-on experiences with gardening and food cultivation allow children to connect the story to real-world applications and discussions about healthy local food:

- **The science of gardening.** Science of gardening lessons can address the basics of what it takes for a plant to grow. This includes visuals of roots and discussions about water, nutrition, and aeration. We discuss why certain things we eat grow underground, while with other plants we eat the leaves, stem, or fruit. Children can then explore these ideas with experiments using soil and seeds.

- **Bugs in the garden.** We shift our focus to the most common bugs we see in our location. For us, this includes ladybugs, a variety of caterpillars, Japanese beetles, bees, and pill bugs (also called roly polies). We can talk about whether these insects are friends, foes, or both and why this may be the case. We also can discuss the importance of pollinators.
- **Composting and garden recycling.** We show and talk about what is in compost and why it is important while relating it back to the science of growing plants. We discuss ways recycling occurs in the garden, such as using old jugs as watering cans, collecting water for plants, and finding things around the house to use as planters.

Programming should center the inclusion of families, offering carryover activities to encourage children to engage in nature play and exploration at home. This allows the skills and language that have been introduced to take root and grow beyond the program. For example, we can give families the supplies they need to develop a potted garden at home: planters, soil, starter plants, watering cans, and fertilizer.

Using Diverse Children's Books

Educators can leverage diverse books to enhance play and exploration in nature in various ways. Incorporating literature into outdoor activities not only enriches the learning experience but also promotes a deeper understanding of diversity and the environment. The following are some ways that I love to unite diverse books with outdoor learning.

Select Diverse Books with Nature Themes

Choose children's books that not only celebrate diversity but also have nature as a central theme. Look for stories that feature characters from various backgrounds engaging with and appreciating nature. Be sure the books selected include not only diverse images but also diverse perspectives and are written by authors from a variety of backgrounds. Remember that nature-themed books can encompass a variety of topics, from constellations to bugs to trees to outdoor recreation. Ensure that the ideas have range and depth, including both familiar topics that relate to what children can do or see regularly as well as topics and experiences that are not currently familiar but may be a part of their plans years down the road. For example, include a book on skiing even if you never see snow and there are no mountains where you are, and connect the idea of skiing to a discussion around seasons and their social aspects.

Outdoor Storytelling Sessions

Sometimes it is not feasible to be in nature or have a full nature-based activity. Restraints and challenges such as time and weather may hinder regular engagement with nature. Conduct reading activities outdoors or adjacent to the outdoors, such as reading under a tree or near a natural setting or intentionally opening a window during reading time.

Nature Exploration Activities

Integrate hands-on nature exploration activities inspired by the themes of diverse books. For example, if a book features characters planting a garden, educators can organize a gardening activity through which children can experience planting seeds and watching them grow.

Multisensory Experiences

Create multisensory experiences by incorporating elements from diverse books into outdoor activities. This can include using props related to the story, playing music that complements the setting, or introducing natural scents and textures.

Nature Journaling and Reflection

Introduce nature journaling as a reflective activity. After reading a diverse book with a nature theme, encourage children to express their thoughts and feelings through drawing, writing, or other creative means in their nature journals. Even the youngest children can develop these reflections. Support each child by allowing them to provide reflections in a way that is comfortable and easy for them.

Nature offers a dynamic and immersive learning environment that naturally complements the development of language and literacy skills in children. By capitalizing on the inherent richness of the outdoors, educators and parents can create opportunities for children to explore, express, and expand their language capabilities. Integrating nature into language and literacy education not only enhances academic skills but also instills a love for learning that is deeply rooted in the natural world.

Reflection Questions

1. How might exposure to stories featuring varied cultural perspectives affect a child's connection to the natural world?
2. How might stories from diverse children's literature centered on nature influence a child's sense of environmental stewardship and responsibility?
3. How does representation in children's literature, particularly in stories about nature, contribute to a child's sense of identity and belonging, especially for those from underrepresented backgrounds?
4. In what ways can interactions with nature, such as exploring gardens or observing wildlife, foster vocabulary development and communication skills in learners?
5. How does engaging with nature encourage storytelling and imaginative play?

References

Stechyson, Natalie. 2019. "Kids' Books Still Have a Lack-of-Diversity Problem, Powerful Image Shows." *HuffPost,* June 21. www.huffpost.com/entry/diversity-kids-books-statistics_l_61087501e4b0497e67026f1c.

SECTION III

Nature Anywhere and Everywhere

IN 2016 I became a Chicago Public Schools classroom teacher and proud card-carrying member of the Chicago Teachers Union. While I had been an educator for years prior, this would be my first experience working in a public school. I worked at a neighborhood school that welcomes students from the surrounding Little Village and Pilsen neighborhoods. The Little Village neighborhood, located in the South Lawndale area of Chicago, is home to a majority Mexican immigrant population. At this school I taught a group of twenty preschool-aged children ages four to five who were of Mexican and Mexican American heritage. It was by chance that the school I worked at had a community-built nature playground about two blocks away. As someone who loves nature and looks for every chance to incorporate it into my students' learning, I took my class there as often as I could. My principal was open to letting us go twice a week for a few hours at a time, which is rare for administrators who are pressed by the school district to show evidence of "rigorous" learning environments.

As I began to take the children more and more to this nature playground, I noticed a stark difference in the way the children played there compared to how they played on the traditional playground in front of the school. We visited the bright blue plastic slides and swings every day, sometimes twice a day. At the traditional playground, there seemed to be more conflicts and conflict language among the children during their play than at the nature playground or even in my classroom. "Noooo!" "Staaaahhp!" and "Teacher!" were common. I noticed that I spent most of my time at the traditional playground resolving conflicts, helping children overcome hurt feelings, and preventing fights. In contrast, play at the nature playground tended to be more language focused and pretend-play oriented. I also observed that I was not spending much time, if any, resolving conflicts. My interest in nature play developed from these informal observations. Yet I also wondered whether it was my bias toward nature that led me to see more positive interactions among the children at the nature playground.

The following school year, 2017–2018, I took my informal observations and turned them into a formal action research project as part of a cohort of Chicago Public Schools educators interested in taking a closer look at how their students learned. I wanted to discover whether my observations had been a result of my own wishful perceptions or if they pointed to a measurable difference in how children play. Over the course of the fall and winter, I collected video segments, each approximately two minutes long, showing the children playing in the three environments: the nature playground, the classroom, and the traditional playground. I followed three case study students in the three spaces and transcribed the videos to document interactions of these children and any other children who became involved in the play. I coded the children's language and categorized based on what I heard in the videos. The four categories were minimal language, conflict language, cooperative language, and pretend play language.

Minimal language happened when the children were vocalizing, screaming, or yelling while running or playing. Conflict language featured the children arguing or yelling at each other to stop. Cooperative language meant the children were working together for a common goal. For example, one video segment showed two children talking to each other to coordinate picking up a large log at the nature playground. Finally, pretend-play language was language the children used to develop a scenario and carry out their premise. One example of this was when three girls were playing on a large hollowed-out log. The log, lying on its side as a sort of tunnel, was about six feet in diameter, and the children had to use smaller logs to climb to the top. In this situation, two of the girls were on top of the log and one of the other girls was trying to get up to join them.

Sofia: I'm the mom, OK? You're the sister, you're the sister.

Ana: I can't! Sister, help me. I'm slipping.

Sofia: I've got you, my baby *(helping Ana climb up onto the log)*. Go, my baby.

Ana: I'm too small too. Mommy, how could I sleep?

Sofia: *Con mami* up here, down there. Grab on here *(holds out a branch)*, grab on here.

Ana: No, I'm . . . Teacher Fong, I'm scared. I can't get down.

Sofia: Lookit. Put your *pie aquí, una [sic] pie. Esta, para aquí.* OK, come on.

Ana: Ah, uh *(climbing up).*

Sofia: Put your *mano aquí (indicates branch).*

Teacher: Slide, there you go—slide, slide. Good job.

Ana: Oh, I did it! I knew I wasn't scared.

Children on log

On another occasion, these same girls were involved in an interaction at the traditional playground that clearly exhibited conflict with minimal language. Ana was at the top of the slide and blocking the way for Sofia to climb up.

Sofia *(climbs up the slide and reaches the top where Ana is standing)*: Ahhhh, she's pushing me! *(Ana pushes Sofia with her foot).* Ahhhhh!

Children on slide

Sofia repeatedly attempted to get to the very top of the slide and through to the other side, and Ana blocked every attempt. That was the totality of speech during the two-minute video.

My findings were remarkable. Approximately 50 percent of the language I observed at the traditional playground was minimal language and 27 percent was conflict language. Cooperative language accounted for 8 percent of the language, and 15 percent was pretend play.

The opposite was true at the nature playground: 44 percent of the language I captured was pretend play and 44 percent cooperative language, while only 8 percent was minimal language and 19 percent conflict language (some language was coded into multiple categories).

The classroom results were also compelling, with 40 percent minimal language and 30 percent conflict language. Surprisingly, only 15 percent was cooperative language, and, luckily for my sense of skill as an educator, 30 percent of the language was pretend play (again, with some language coded into multiple categories).

In the middle of an urban environment, a small (approximately three thousand square foot) lot provided enough nature to inspire the use of complex language in my students. Pretend play and cooperative language require executive functioning skills, planning, social skills, and empathy. If you've ever played a game that required you to create an impromptu story with another adult, you know how difficult pretend play in the moment can be.

David Sobel and Julie Ernst (2023) conducted a study with Head Start students and found that even some incorporation of "nature-based practices" positively affects the resilience and executive functioning skills of young children. What was most startling about their findings is that more nature-based practices did not seem to have a greater effect on the children's resilience and executive functioning skills. The authors write, "Some nature is better than no nature, but a lot of nature is not necessarily better than some nature" (Sobel and Ernst 29).

These findings mean that any nature space, no matter the size, has the potential to positively impact the development of young children. My conclusions and those of many other researchers seem to agree. While as educators and parents we strive to match our children's experience to the idyllic images of children wandering happily through natural forest land in the latest outdoor gear, the research would suggest that such experiences have no greater value for children than time spent outside in simple coats and hats, playing in a six-foot-wide patch of soil between the fence and concrete pad of the playground at their public school playground. While I strongly advocate for as much access

Children playing in patch of soil

to nature as possible for children of color, we can also support educators and families to use whatever nature they have, however big or small, and know that they will experience similar benefits.

The stories in section 3 call on us to engage with nature right outside our doors and even inside our homes. Courtney Newby tells us how she found nature—or rather, how nature found her—and taught her new lessons in working with children. Dr. Deja Jones holds space for the stories of her Black students in nature. Suzette Salmon uses poetry to share how she came to terms with the parts of nature that she didn't always love. And lastly, Jasmin Field shows us how a backyard can transform into a magical place to explore nature.

Reflection Questions

1. In your work with children, have you observed differences in their play while in different indoor and outdoor spaces? If so, what factors influence these differences in behavior?

2. Were you surprised by the findings of Sobel and Ernst that some access to nature has the same benefits as more access to nature? Explain.

3. What is one wondering or question you have about the children you work with? How can you design a simple study to delve into this question and provide you with insight into these children?

References

Sobel, David, and Julie Ernst. 2023. "Some Nature Is Better Than No Nature: A Review of Research on Nature-Based Early Childhood Education." *Exchange Press*, 46 (3): 26–31.

CHAPTER 9

Mother Nature Reclaimed Me

Courtney Newby, Seekonk, MA

Courtney Newby has been an early childhood educator for more than twenty years. She earned her bachelor's degree in early childhood education from Rhode Island College and is currently a Level 1 certified nature-based educator. Courtney has a strong passion for teaching our youngest learners and has a particular interest in social-emotional learning through engagement with nature.

As a young child growing up in Alabama, I was immersed in nature. Helping on my caregivers' farm, feeding the animals and harvesting crops. Playing outside for hours on end, unlocking secrets of nature through play. Patiently waiting until the sun set so I could catch fireflies in a mason jar. I loved playing in nature, and it was all I knew until I was eight and moved up north to Rhode Island, where play for me would change completely. I was still playing outside, but playing outside in the city is vastly different from playing outside in the country. Finding joy in nature would escape me for decades.

My journey to becoming an educator was not linear. I traveled many roads until finally I realized that I was meant to be in the classroom. I started working as a teacher's assistant when I was nineteen years old. In the years that followed, I pursued a degree in criminal justice, had my two daughters, realized criminal justice wasn't the path I wanted to take, and even looked into careers in the medical field. Although at the time I felt that nothing was working out for me, unbeknownst to me, Mother Nature was drawing me closer.

Finally, years later, I obtained my bachelor's degree in early childhood education and eventually found myself as a lead teacher in a preschool three-year-old classroom. It was then that science started to pique my interest. I began holding what I called Science Fridays, which included various science experiments and outdoor experiences. New England has beautiful foliage in the fall, so I would take my preschoolers on walks to look for signs of fall, observe trees changing colors, and feel the brisk air on our skin. I was content, or so I thought, until 2020 came and changed my life again.

In the field of nature-based education, a *sit spot* refers to a specific place in nature where children as well as adults regularly go to sit quietly and observe the natural surroundings. It's a deliberate and mindful practice aimed at deepening one's connection with nature. Educators guide children to understand sit spots as well as gain the skills to sit and observe using all their senses. Sit spots help children understand the interaction between the creatures in nature and their ecosystems over time. Sit spots also foster awareness, contemplation, and learning via direct observation of the natural world.

In March 2020, the world shut down for COVID-19, and so did I, both mentally and physically. I became stuck, unable to do easy everyday tasks. I thought I would snap out of it until the death of George Floyd in May, which made my situation worse. I tried not to watch TV or go on social media. I began taking walks in nature, bringing a blanket with me to sit and observe nature and all its beauty. Nature was helping me, and I felt a renewed calmness.

When I was at home, I felt like my walls were caving in on me. I needed to do something to make my home feel like nature so I could feel that calmness on rainy days or days when I didn't have the strength to leave my house. So I bought houseplants. Every time I had a bad day I would buy a plant; some days I would buy two or three. Researching and caring for plants began to heal me—or as I like to think of it, Mother Nature was reclaiming me.

In August 2020, I returned to work. I was informed that I would only be outside for an hour in the morning and an hour in the late afternoon. I was also informed that I would not be able to go on walks because I would be alone in my classroom due to low enrollment. I worked eight hours a day and was indoors for six hours. This confinement literally made me sick. But at least I had big, beautiful windows in my classroom, so I went to the store and bought more plants. I took clippings from plants I had at home and propagated them, teaching my preschoolers all about the process. On Science Fridays, I would ask a question, the children would make a prediction, and we would do a simple experiment. After the experiment, we would discuss what happened and why. The children brought me so much joy, but being stuck indoors did not.

In April 2021, I found out that the Wheeler School was looking for an early childhood education teacher. The beautiful campus, called the Nest, sits on 120 acres with trails, ponds, and fields. Lots of thoughts ran through my head. I felt self-doubt, wondering whether I was good enough to teach at the school. I was used to teaching in an urban setting, primarily working with other people of color except for the administration. I felt uneasy going into an environment where there were few educators who looked like me. I felt like I would have to prove myself the second I walked through the door and had to give 110 percent just to be deemed all right. I also felt self-doubt creeping in because I didn't have much knowledge or experience about nature from an educator's perspective. Although I loved exploring nature with young learners, I wasn't sure if I had the right skills or background to teach it in a formal way. Yet my joy and passion for the outdoors made the nature-based preschool a perfect fit for me, and I got the job.

Even though I had been teaching for over twenty years at this point, when I started at Wheeler I felt like a novice. The fact was, I knew nothing formal about nature-based education, and I felt I had to prove myself because I was the only Black educator on this campus. I needed to show that I was a good educator and deserved to be in this space, so to begin with I fell back on what I knew: In my previous years teaching, I had conducted a tree study with my preschoolers, and we walked around the neighborhood near our school and observed different kinds of trees. So that would be the first formal lesson I taught at the Nest.

One thing I knew for sure was that I needed to learn more about the natural world, and fast. My coteacher, Michelle, was amazing, and I learned so much from her my first year, but I needed to learn more. Michelle suggested I take a summer 2022 course with the Eastern Region Association of Forest and Nature Schools (ERAFANS). Although I wasn't excited to take a class during my first-ever summer off, I agreed because I wanted to learn more about the natural world. The text we used for the course was *Coyote's Guide to Connecting with Nature* by Jon Young, Ellen Haas, and Evan McGown. One of my first take-aways from this book was not to look at myself as a teacher when outdoors, but rather as a mentor. I needed to mentor the children, find which aspects of nature brought them joy, and expand upon those. *Coyote's Guide* mentions Joseph Cornell's Flow Learning model for outdoor education. The model goes as follows: Create enthusiasm, focus attention, direct experience, and gather/share inspiration. I had already done some of this during my first year teaching at the Wheeler School. My previous self-doubt slowly began to fade.

During this course I learned so much, and I also realized that I was in my place doing exactly what I was meant to do: mentoring children in nature. I was in my quiet sit spot when I had this epiphany.

I looked up at the clouds and mouthed, "Thank you, Mother Nature." Through all the turmoil I felt during my first year teaching at the Nest, she came to remind me that she was watching, and all of this was a learning process.

I would be remiss if I didn't mention that there were very few people of color in the ERAFANS course with me. My friends would joke with me about being a "nature person," like it was some foreign concept to them. None of my colleagues looked like me. I felt alone. But nonetheless, being in nature and teaching in and about nature was bringing me joy. That joy unlocked an intellectual gift in me that I didn't know I had: the ability to take emergent curriculum and create multidisciplinary lessons for my classroom.

In the fall of 2022, I returned to work feeling enthusiastic and energized. I was going to let the children's interests lead me in deciding what to teach. Emergent curriculum was perfect because the children and I would learn together. I brought a journal with me to write anecdotal observations about the children. The children often stopped me because they had found something cool they wanted me to see—like the time there were small pink balls growing

In essence, emergent curriculum emerges from the interaction between the learner, the environment, and the educators within a given context or setting. The curricula, or the learning experiences, emerge from learners' questions, curiosities, and ideas. Educators reflect frequently on the learners' words, actions, and material use and develop learning experiences that engage the learners deeper into that particular topic of interest. This approach emphasizes flexibility and responsiveness to the unique needs and curiosities of the learners involved. The learners and educators engage in multiple cycles of inquiry, working together to make meaning of the world around them.

on a log. Eve said, "Why is there bubblegum growing on a tree?" I quickly took a picture and told Eve I would research what it was and get back to them. We as a class learned that it was called wolf's-milk slime mold, and we could recognize it from that point on.

Eve discovering wolf's-milk slime mold on a log during outdoor exploration

Something I especially love about being a mentor to children in nature is seeing how each child finds their niche. Some children love to dig for worms or bugs. Others like imaginative play using nature items as props. Then you have the builders and climbers who love exercising their gross-motor skills to get things done. In nature, children are allowed the freedom to choose what they want to do and learn. In the same way I found joy in nature, the children also found joy in nature in their own ways. In the words of Gholdy Muhammad (2023), in nature the children "unlock their genius." I saw children using critical thinking skills and spatial awareness, showing empathy, and boosting their self-esteem and that of their fellows. Watching the children I mentor in nature is also healing to me. When I am in nature, I don't feel the heaviness of the world. Every day I find something magical about Mother Nature, and that brings me joy.

I am happy that Mother Nature reclaimed me. She has allowed me to defy stereotypes. People of color *do* belong in nature; our ancestors lived in nature. I may be one of the few educators of color these children have in their lifetime. Even if they don't remember me, I want them to remember the joy they felt in nature. If they are like me and happen to drift away from nature, I hope Mother Nature comes and reclaims them too. When life gets hard, they can go outdoors and find that childhood joy when their problems don't exist, even if it's only for a few minutes. I also hope that the children I mentor in nature share their knowledge and most importantly their joy with others, especially students of color. I don't want them to feel different or awkward for being a nature lover. I want the joy they experience while in nature to shine so brightly that others will want to find that joy too.

Our Stories

I love children's spontaneity when they play in nature. A new world awakens in them. I love being an observer during this play. I also love when the children show me an item in nature that has sparked their interest. I carry so many of these stories in my heart.

Dre

Dre exploring the characteristics of a root

Dre loved to dig and find the roots of plants and trees. One day I went over to him and asked what roots do to help trees. He responded. "That's easy, they give it food and hold it in the ground." To scaffold his learning, I said, "I wonder if the roots do anything else." He shrugged his shoulders. I did some research and found that some scientists believe that forests communicate through roots! I was so excited to share that fact with the children, especially Dre, because his memory was impeccable, and I knew that he would share this knowledge with his peers outside of school.

Cali

While in the woods one day, Cali found a salamander that wasn't moving and put it in a cup. We noted that it was really cold outside. I asked Cali, "What do you think happens to salamanders in the cold?" Cali didn't know and neither did I, so I looked it up. Salamanders become lethargic in the cold. My coteacher suggested that Cali blow in the cup to warm up the salamander, and like magic, the salamander started moving.

Cali blowing warm air into observation cup and watching the salamander inside come alive

Left: RJ smiling with leaves he found while on a nature walk
Right: EmmaSofia observing a worm

RJ

RJ found a piece of a plant while on a hike. He kept this plant with him during lunch, and after lunch he began to use the plant in his sociodramatic play. In the beginning of his play, he just looked and it and observed the leaves and stem. He held the plant in his hand while he engaged with other students in the class. During his play, RJ came up to me and said, "Look, Ms. Newby, I'm Mother Nature and the plant is growing from me!" This piece of a plant brought RJ so much joy. RJ did not verbalize why, but the joy on his face was undeniable.

EmmaSofia

EmmaSofia was observing a worm, trying to figure out whether it was one of the Asian jumping worms we had been studying. She noticed that it was smaller, the color was different, and it didn't have the band that jumping worms have on their body. We did some research together and learned that juvenile jumping worms don't have the band and are a reddish-brown color like the worm in her hand, so she could have been right!

Gratitude

At the end of each playtime in nature my class takes a moment to gather in a circle and give gratitude to Mother Nature. Sometimes it is a simple "Thank you, Mother Nature." Other times, each child tells Mother Nature what they are grateful for. This allows children to think about what they played with in nature on this particular day. Sometimes I ask open-ended questions to encourage the children to dive deeper. It is my hope for the children to pass on this love they have for Mother Nature and that later, during tough times in their lives, they may recall these amazing, healing memories.

Courtney and a group of children showing gratitude to Mother Nature

Reflection Questions

1. What is a meaningful experience you've had in nature that has shaped your perspective, and how does it continue to influence your relationship with the natural world?
2. As an educator, what key lessons or values do you hope the children you teach will carry with them from their experiences in nature?
3. What aspects of nature bring you joy, and how do they influence your overall well-being and perspective on life?
4. What hesitations, if any, do you have about teaching in nature, and how do these concerns shape your approach to outdoor education? What experiences or beliefs contribute to these feelings, and how might addressing them enhance your teaching practice and the learning experiences of your students?

References

Muhammad, Gholdy. 2023. "Cultivating Genius: Joy, Equity, and Educational Excellence." Conference presentation. NAIS People of Color Conference, St. Louis, Missouri, November 30.

CHAPTER 10

Stories from Black Childhoods in Nature

Deja L. Jones, Newark, NJ

Deja L. Jones, PhD, is an educator, founder, and head of school at Honeypot Montessori in Newark, New Jersey, where she curates nature experiences for children ages three to six. With a decade of experience spanning roles from former journalist to classroom teacher, she seamlessly blends her passions for education and storytelling. Driven by a commitment to empowering Black children, Deja's research delves into critical issues such as environmental racism and resilience in early childhood development.

I GREW UP IN Trenton, New Jersey, an urban city that has seemed to deteriorate as I've gotten older. What I looked forward to most as a child was spending summers taking family trips to North Carolina. My grandma's family lived in Willow Springs, North Carolina, a small rural town that has gone through a redevelopment process in the years since my childhood. After spending time there, we'd load the family van and travel to Pamlico, North Carolina, an even smaller coastal town. I remember doing things during my summers in North Carolina that I didn't experience in New Jersey. My family owned acres of land in North Carolina, and I remember running around the fields with cousins, playing tag and hide-and-seek, our bare feet sliding around in the lush grass and mud. We'd dig holes in the moist dirt and try to catch the frogs that hopped out. We'd go on adventures through abandoned fields and homes to see what we could find. My great-grandma owned chickens and had a coop in her backyard, and sometimes, they'd get out and wander around the lawn.

Southern values lived within my family and carried over into my Northern upbringing; however, with the demands of city life, work, and school, being outside and enjoying outside time looked very different. Being in touch with nature meant finding space to run up and down the sidewalk and street with the other neighborhood kids, playing games of freeze tag until we were tired,

Note: The contents of this chapter are based on a dissertation research study.
Jones, Deja L. 2023. "Sticks & Stones and Roots & Bones: A Narrative Inquiry Study on Black Children's Cultural Engagement in Nature." PhD diss., Saybrook University. Proquest (30989774).

Children on a log

or riding our bikes to the park and coming home with leaves we collected. But whether we are raised in an urban or rural setting, when we miss that foundation at a young age, that lesson of our reciprocal relationship with nature and animals, we become oriented to a world where we don't view ourselves as part of a natural ecosystem.

In a world that increasingly gravitates toward screens and concrete jungles, the call of the wild remains as relevant as ever, especially for young children. Nature is an invaluable teacher, imparting vital lessons about life, interconnectedness, and the deep-rooted relationship between humanity and the environment. Yet the benefits of nature experiences extend far beyond biology or ecology. They encompass an intricate web of cultural, emotional, and spiritual connections that profoundly impact the lives of children, particularly those from Black communities. In this chapter, we delve into the heart of these connections, exploring the effects on Black children of having meaningful and regular encounters with nature and how nature serves as an essential cultural connection.

Building Stories Using Narrative Inquiry

For my dissertation study exploring Black children's cultural experiences in nature, I carefully selected Black children from diverse backgrounds, ensuring a robust array of experiences. Their age and where they came from were vital aspects to consider, as these factors would bring different narratives. We engaged in heartfelt interviews, during which they expressed their experiences in their own words. To add color and depth to our narrative, I encouraged the children to use artwork and other expressive forms to share their feelings and thoughts.

During data analysis, I looked for patterns, recurring themes, common structures, and shared metaphors woven into the children's stories. My goal was to collect data and breathe life into these stories, understanding them within the broader context of society and culture. Black children's stories, unique perspectives, and insights were in the spotlight. This approach to analyzing data resulted in more inclusive conversations about their relationship with the natural world. The experiences of Black children in nature aren't isolated but rather deeply connected to their cultural heritage, family dynamics, and local environments.

Preconceived notions and biases can be challenged by authentic stories directly from the mouths of Black children. These narratives provided a nuanced, accurate portrayal of their natural experiences, dispelling misconceptions and stereotypes. By pinpointing barriers to access, we pave the way for targeted interventions that can bridge the gaps that currently exist in research and programming. Some of these gaps include a lack of representation of children of color in nature and nature education, a lack of cultural relevancy in how educators engage children of color in nature education, and research studies that take a deficit approach to Black engagement in nature, which in turn make that engagement invisible. By honoring their narratives, we pave the way for a more equitable and enriching relationship between Black communities and the natural world.

Outdoor art

In my daily encounters with my storyteller participants, each session commenced with an art exploration inspired by nature. Using an array of colored markers, pencils, and crayons, the children worked to capture their unique perceptions of nature. Their illustrations portrayed the natural world's beauty and the activities they cherished, the people who shared those experiences, and their aspirations for a nature-infused community.

These art sessions were a prelude to engaging discussions about the children's perspectives on nature. Delving into their thoughts, we explored the significance of their nature experiences, unraveling the lessons they gleaned while immersed in the great outdoors. The dialogue provided a rich insight into nature's profound impact on their young lives.

My role as a researcher, writer, and educator extended beyond that of observer. During our time together, I often assumed the position of a silent spectator, allowing the children's natural inclinations to unfold organically. However, there were moments when I became an active participant, seamlessly blending into their world. I found myself digging holes to construct miniature landscapes, collecting leaves for an ant amusement park, and following the enthusiastic guidance of a seven-year-old mentor, learning the art of tree climbing.

Aimee

I met Aimee, age six, at her home in urban New Jersey, and she was immediately eager to start creating her art reflection about what nature looks like for her. Through Aimee's stories, I learned that her nature experiences sometimes happened away from her home. She had just finished doing twirls and spins in her glittery pink dress as we sat in her colorfully decorated concrete backyard. She played with her dolls and pretended her mom's plant collection was a jungle. She recalled camping trips with her family and all the wonderful things they did:

> *I'm going to Georgia to go camping with my family. I go with a lot of people. I went with my aunties and my cousins. The last time I went, we planted flowers and two trees and went to a waterfall. I wasn't scared when I saw the waterfall, so we played in the water. I got all wet, and it was a little cold. We put up a tent and made a big fire for roasting marshmallows.*

Semaj

I met Semaj, age seven, at a national park in rural Virginia. As we walked into the park, the first thing Semaj noticed was a large tree amid all the high grass and a sprinkling of thinner trees. He declared he would climb that tree and teach others how to do so:

> *My name is Semaj, and I am going to show you how to climb a tree!*

Semaj dashed for one of the tallest trees with his little sister close behind. He gave us a step-by-step tutorial that got him and his sister onto the first thick branch of the tree.

> *You have to make sure you put your foot into the cracks in the trunk and then pull yourself up.*

He demonstrated by stepping onto a thick root at the tree trunk and pressing his other foot on top of a small stump sticking out of the trunk, declaring, "Climbing trees is easy!" He maneuvered his way back onto the ground and helped his little sister down before they ran off to dig holes in the dirt.

Digging in the soil

Samuel

I met Samuel, age five, and his older sister, Sasha, at a park in urban New Jersey. As his mother unstrapped him from his car seat and helped him out of the car, he immediately ran for the playground. He called out, "Come on, guys, let's play!" to a group of children he spotted as he dashed for the blue and white playground with tall castles and sliding houses. It was a small, gated play zone in the park surrounded by acres of natural greenery. Along with the other children, Samuel created an obstacle course using the playground equipment: they took turns going down the slide, climbing across the monkey bars without falling and getting eaten by the giant alligators, and seeing who could make the tire swing go the highest and spin the fastest. The sounds of the children screaming and laughing fused with the sounds of house music and the steady roar of the food truck just outside the gate.

Sasha

Walking into one of the largest parks in urban New Jersey, Sasha, age eight, ignored the sounds of sirens rushing down the avenue past the buildings that stood across the street from the vast greenness of the park. This nature space divided the neighborhood; whereas one side was completely urban and lined with subsidized housing, the far side of the park faced large, pristine homes. In the parking lot, Sasha gravitated toward the wooden guardrails and used them as a balance beam before making her way to the top of a hill. Standing facing the sky, she lay in the grass with her arms and legs extended. She yelled about wanting to feel the sun on her face even though the weather was dark and overcast as the clouds swelled with pending rain. She recalled a time she saw a rainbow at the park while enjoying ice cream with her dad and grandma:

> *I've seen a rainbow, maybe about three times; probably more, but this one time, when I was getting ice cream with my dad and grandma, we saw one at the park.*

Kenya and Xia

I met Kenya, age eight, at a park in urban New York City. She arrived in a car with her older sister Xia, age nine, infant sister, and their mom. Kenya described nature in her neighborhood as looking less like trees and forest and more like concrete pavement and neighborhood playgrounds, where she loves to carry a soccer ball and teach her sisters how to do flips. She stated,

> *I learned how to do backflips and gymnastics. I run around with my sisters and teach them how to do flips in the park.*

On what Kenya named "family nature days," Kenya and Xia help their mom and dad pack up the family truck and drive to a larger park with hiking trails, dog walks, and a river where they see boats and ferries on the water. The girls have spotted a red cardinal nesting inside a pine tree while exploring the park.

Xia, age nine, never considered herself a nature girl until she was hiking with her mom and younger sisters and discovered a cave. Taking family hikes along the trail to the secret cave became Xia's favorite thing to do with her sisters:

> *There's this cave we go to by the hiking trail. It's a long hill and then the cave at the end. Mommy lets us go and play in there but always tells us to make good choices. Sometimes we have to run out if there are too many bugs.*

Hailey

After I met Hailey, age seven, in suburban Virginia, she took me on a journey through her backyard garden, where she plants all the wonderful vegetables she likes to eat, such as carrots. Living in a suburban community, Hailey understands the importance of living things and having quality shelters to keep them safe:

> *Last year, I made a hotel for caterpillars at my grandma's house with my friends. We had to make it in the dirt so the sticks could stay up. We used sticks, rocks, and leaves for the beds. I think they enjoyed their new home.*

As summer approached, Hailey liked to watch the fireflies light up at night in her backyard and told a story about a time when her class learned a song about fireflies.

How We Play: Assessing the Findings

Each child painted a picture of how they like to experience nature where they live, some of the challenges they face, and some of their fears and even their desires for nature. Our sessions culminated with the unbridled joy of free play. Positioned at the intersection of researcher and playmate, I witnessed the children's imaginative processes unfold. From observing superhero gatherings atop playground equipment to participating in daring escapades down slides to thwart imaginary villains, these moments were not just play but integral

Children rock hopping

components of the research journey. Amid laughter and shared adventures, the essence of childhood and the profound connections between nature and imagination became evident, shaping a narrative that transcended the boundaries of conventional research. Conversations with these youngsters revealed distinct patterns in their relationship with the natural world.

Theme 1: Learning in Nature with Family and Peers

Children described their favorite nature experiences with close relatives and friends. In response to the question "Do you have a favorite person you like to experience nature with?" all the children named a family member or friend as their favorite person to engage in nature with, and many of their nature experiences took place close to that person's home (if it was not their own). For example, Aimee spoke of her mom and her friend:

> *Me and Mommy go camping, and we roast marshmallows, and she reads me stories and we put up a tent. The last time I went camping, me and my friend went to a waterfall.*

Hailey spoke of creative play with her best friend that included making a "home" for small critters and backyard gardening at her grandmother's house:

> *I planted carrots in my grandma's backyard. We have lots of seeds and plants, lots of things. My favorite is peas. Sometimes I help my mom pick the vegetables for dinner.*

Children with siblings noted the differences between their nature play styles. For example, Sasha compared her exploration of nature to that of her younger brother:

> *I like to explore nature with my little brother. He likes to run around a lot. I run with him sometimes, but sometimes I get tired and don't want to run anymore. I like to have picnics in the park, though. I bring bananas, strawberries, oranges, apples, and a notebook to draw and color pictures.*

Children in the study who had a sibling spoke of teaching each other how to do things in nature, such as Kenya teaching her sisters how to do gymnastics in the park or Semaj teaching his younger sister how to climb a tree properly.

Parents' connection to nature also played a big role in how and what their children learned about nature, regardless of physical access. Throughout the study, I gathered background information about parents' activities in nature that included coordinating local hiking groups, teaching outdoor yoga and meditation in the park, working at community gardens, and coleading outdoor and forest school learning pods and homeschools. For example, Xia discussed things she and her siblings learned from their mom during a homeschool science lesson, which often included nature exploration with her sisters:

> *At home we learned about habitats and did a project on where we used shoeboxes, and I think that's nature too. I did the rainforest, and my sister did the ocean. I learned there's a lot of animals and different types of rainforests across the world. There's some that have tropical animals and don't have rain. There's some that have a little bit of rain and grow fruit trees, and there's some where it rains all the time. I learned that in rainforests, certain animals live in different parts of the trees.*

Xia's homeschool experiences were not just about her and her siblings learning about nature but also an example of how adults who regularly engage and care about nature can influence children's thoughts and ideas about their own engagement with nature.

Theme 2: Using Games and Media to Learn About Nature

Half of the children in the study spoke of education technology when discussing their experiences with nature. For example, Semaj played a mobile game, *Plants vs. Zombies*, to learn about nature concepts. He described how the PBS Kids series *Wild Kratts* exposed him to many types of animals. Semaj talked about some of the animals he became familiar with through the show and stated how he learned to take care of animals, which is an example of higher-level learning:

> *I learn to take care of animals. I can take care of animals by cleaning up all the trash outside and not litter. My favorite TV show is Wild Kratts. I learn about all types of animals and bugs. I learn about lions, badgers, leopards, rabbits, and stingrays. Oh, and don't forget about the pandas and red pandas too. We can keep animals safe by keeping them where they are.*

While many environmental researchers and educators aim to encourage children to experience the outdoors more, some children with limited outside access have found ways to engage with nature via computer applications and games like *Plants vs. Zombies.* Semaj related some of the video game characters to their real-life inspiration:

> *I know that plants can help you survive if zombies come. In the game, there's pea shooters that's related to pea pods. Venus Flytrap is a character and Kernel Corn. And the Night Cap ninjas are related to mushrooms.*

In *Plants vs. Zombies*, Semaj experienced plant life personified as blurbs about each character popped up on the screen. For example, he mentioned the peashooter, a character who shoots out peas to kill the zombies. He learned about aspects of nature, including an awareness of how the video character functions mimic actual plant functions. For peashooters to survive, they need lots of sunlight, carbon dioxide, and water, much like real-life pea plants. He also spoke of the character Venus Flytrap, which captures and traps the zombies within his jaws and can heal himself, much like how real-life Venus flytraps heal themselves by consuming the nutrients of small creatures. While many nature initiatives encourage children to get outdoors for play, having access to media technologies can also increase awareness and exposure to nature education. These experiences encourage children to unlock a level of mental creativity and imagination that uses the reality of nature as a tool for fantasy immersion.

Fairy house

Theme 3: Using Nature for Make-Believe Fantasy Play

For two children, nature served as a backdrop to their fantasy play. Being in nature allowed them to explore their favorite superheroes and create games. Samuel told a story of his make-believe play with his mother:

> *One time me and my mommy played a game where we went camping in the jungle, and it was raining. We were in the tent when we saw a giant lion. My mommy jumped out and screamed at the lion so that it could go away, and we went back to our camping trip and pretended to roast marshmallows.*

On the playground, Samuel led a game of Batman and Spider-Man with a group of neighborhood kids he had just met. They ran up hills in the park and used a children's playhouse replica of a medieval castle as their superhero headquarters to discuss what they would do to all the villains when they captured them.

Xia loved dancing to her favorite songs in the fields at her neighborhood park, fantasizing about flowers that do not actually exist there:

> *I picture myself dancing in the fields and picking flowers. I'm dancing in a field of roses, daisies, and all types of other flowers. I wish we had more flowers in my neighborhood. I would plant them.*

Theme 4: Fears About Nature

All eight of the children in this study described moments when they felt fear while having a nature experience or named animals or insects they were afraid of. Still, these fears did not contribute to a lack of interest in or engagement with nature. The children understood that some animals require distance. Kenya listed all her fears about nature:

Harvesting

> *I'm afraid of stepping in poop and bees because even though they're not predators, if you try to play with them and do stuff, they'll attack you. Once my sisters were scaring the bees, but they kept flying to me and I didn't want to get stung.*

Bees were a common fear, referred to by five of the children. Other fears the children mentioned included spiders, poisonous animals and insects, skunks, sharks, grizzly bears, and cockroaches. Aimee said, "I'm afraid of skunks because I hate taking tomato baths. If a skunk sprays you, it's going to be really stinky." Samuel said, "I never seen a shark in real life before, but I'm scared of sharks because they can eat you." The children's fears were not generalized and were tied to specific effects, and the children were still able to enjoy nature.

Theme 5: Experiencing Nature Away from Home

The study's children could identify nature experiences in their communities and share a story of a memorable nature experience away from home. Some of these involved traveling far. Hailey talked about her travels to her grandmother's house and how she does most of her planting when she's there:

Neighborhood safari

> *I like to go to my grandma's house. She lives in a townhouse in Virginia. When I was there one time, we planted a pack of carrot seeds. I like carrots. I like to eat them with mashed potatoes and mac and cheese.*

Samuel's favorite place to see a variety of animals in one place was easily accessible to him:

> *My favorite place to go is the zoo. I like to look and play with some of the animals. I always go to see the giraffes, and I can feed them! I like to see the crocodiles too; they're nice to look at.*

Understanding that nature experiences can be as natural as a beach or as curated as a zoo, children in the study could identify nature or have nature experiences close to home but also in other places and neighborhoods.

Theme 6: Types of Nature Desired in Neighborhoods

All the children in the study had access to nature, whether in their neighborhoods or by traveling farther away. Still, each offered recommendations on how nature could be better where they live, citing the need for cleaner communities, access to nature as a food source, and opportunities for animals to dwell freely. Aimee and Sasha, respectively, wished for more green space creations that would attract butterflies and provide food for the community. Aimee said,

> *I want to see more gardens in my neighborhood so we can have butterflies. I wish I had a pond so I can say hi to the ducks.*

Sasha said,

> *I would like to see more butterflies. More trees. Let's see more grass for the flowers. I want more of the trees with fruit on them like cherries and apples. Those are my favorite things to eat.*

Xia's desire for more nature in her neighborhood began with stewardship practices that included cleanups:

> *I don't see people playing in nature where I live. I think if people didn't litter and cleaned up and be nice to nature, more people would be outside. Nature is like us . . . it needs water and food and to be clean. Lots of people like clean neighborhoods and lots of people want clean neighborhoods.*

Theme 7: Experiencing Nature Through Hobbies

Each of the children in the study shared a story about their favorite things to do while they were in nature. These activities included camping, hiking, picnicking, free play, and gardening. Where Semaj lives, there are natural water systems that he enjoys searching with his sister:

> *We like to play in water a lot and sometimes at the water by my house we like to look for fish. We saw a crayfish in there once. I like to climb trees and teach my sister how to climb trees too.*

Aimee's hobbies in nature consist of cultural activities such as African drumming, among other things:

> *My favorite place to go is outside to the park. I have a park by my house, and I go to an African drumming circle with my friends sometimes in nature. We like to play and run around. Sometimes we climb and sit in the trees. Sometimes I like to read a book.*

Hailey's hobbies in nature showed her love of food and growing foods for her family to enjoy:

I like to plant stuff. My mommy has a garden that I help with. We plant a lot of different vegetables that we cook for dinner. We have peppers, eggplants, tomatoes, spinach, and snap peas. I planted carrots at my grandma's house.

Sasha's family established hiking trips as their activity of choice:

I like to go hiking. We go up to the mountain view. I follow some paths that are different colors like red and yellow and blue. The colors are stickers on the trees that tell us which way to go. We always go to the waterfall. I usually go with my mom and dad to the river flow. I try to fish with a stick, and my mom always scoops up the water to save, and I collect leaves.

Tomato picking

Leaf collecting

Other Findings

The children shared other unique narratives highlighting their experiences and knowledge of nature that did not fit into the common themes listed above. Some children shared narratives that included stewardship characteristics and expressed empathy toward animals, whether through their desire to build shelters for them or calling for stopping product testing on animals. Hailey stated,

If I had a nature clubhouse, I could make cool houses for birds and bugs. I have a perfect spot in my backyard for one. It would be for me so I can make animal shelters.

Semaj offered an environmental solution to ensure animals' safety. He shared,

People need to stop littering because it harms animals. People also should stop making deodorants that make animals die more.

The themes revealed that regardless of Black children's level of engagement or access to nature, they can still create meaningful experiences that teach them how to empathize with animals, explore their desires and fears, and learn from their peers in nature.

What Can We Do to Center Blackness in Nature Experiences?

Centering Black children's experiences in nature and ensuring they have exposure to the natural environment is crucial for their well-being and for fostering their connection to the outdoors. Here are several suggestions for ways to achieve this:

- Ask questions and solicit opinions. Start by actively listening to the perspectives of Black children. Understand their interests, concerns, and aspirations regarding nature. Engage in open conversations to learn about their unique connections and experiences with the outdoors. Too often we miss opportunities to simply ask Black children what they wish to see and what they already know. Involve Black children in the design and planning of outdoor spaces to ensure they are functional and resonate with their needs and interests. This could include community gardens, nature trails, or outdoor classrooms.
- Increase representation in outdoor media and curriculum. Ensure that outdoor media, such as books, TV shows, and online content, feature diverse characters and highlight the experiences of Black children in nature. Representation in media can influence children's perceptions and interests. Develop and promote an inclusive curriculum that incorporates diverse perspectives on nature. Include contributions from Black scientists, environmentalists, and conservationists to showcase various roles within the field.
- Prioritize community partnerships. Collaborate with local community organizations, schools, and leaders to organize nature-focused events, workshops, and programs. Establishing partnerships can help create a supportive and inclusive environment for Black children to explore nature.
- Increase accessible green spaces. Advocate for accessible green spaces in urban areas where Black children may have limited access to nature. Ensure that these spaces are safe, well-maintained, and inclusive. Identify

and address any barriers preventing Black children from engaging in outdoor activities. This could include financial barriers, transportation issues, or safety concerns. Work to create solutions that make outdoor experiences more accessible.

- Offer outdoor education programs. Implement outdoor education programs that specifically target Black children. These programs can include nature walks, camping trips, and hands-on activities that foster a sense of wonder and connection with the natural world. Start early by promoting a love for nature from a young age. Integrate nature-based activities into early childhood education and child care programs, helping Black children develop a lifelong connection to the outdoors.
- Center mentors and family engagement. Introduce Black role models and mentors who have a passion for nature and the outdoors. Positive role models can inspire and guide Black children, encouraging them to explore and appreciate the natural environment. Engage families by organizing nature-based events that cater to the entire family. Encourage parents to participate in outdoor activities with their children to strengthen family bonds and create lasting memories.

Tree ID

Nature cleanup

By implementing these strategies, you can create an inclusive and supportive environment that centers on Black children's natural experiences, fostering a love for the outdoors and a sense of stewardship for the environment.

In environmental education, narrative research studies that actively include and prioritize the experiences of Black children have the transformative power

Binoculars

to illuminate profound insights. By centering these narratives, we gain a nuanced understanding of the intricate relationships between individuals and nature, shedding light on their unique perspectives, challenges, and aspirations. Such studies serve as invaluable tools, not only guiding necessary policy shifts but also presenting opportunities for redesigning educational curricula to be more inclusive, culturally relevant, and responsive to the diverse needs of Black learners. Moreover, the collective impact of these narratives transcends the academic realm, carrying the potential to catalyze broader social change and justice. Through the authentic representation of Black children's experiences in nature, we embark on a journey toward a more equitable and inclusive environmental education landscape, fostering a harmonious relationship between diverse communities and the natural world.

Reflection Questions

1. Think about nature memories from your childhood and where they took place, who was there, and how you felt. How can you create similar experiences for the children in your life?
2. Considering ways to use available outdoor spaces or bring nature indoors, what can we do to help children see themselves as part of nature, even in urban settings?
3. What small changes could you make in your daily routine to give children more time in nature?
4. Think about how diversity in nature experiences can affect children's learning and appreciation of nature. Why is it important to include diverse perspectives in outdoor activities and learning?

CHAPTER 11

Your Yard Is Enough

Suzette Salmon, Chicago, IL

Suzette Salmon, or Miss Sue, is a Chicago-based educator who immigrated from Jamaica. She helps home child care providers overcome burnout and rediscover their passion for educating. Her hands-on approach blends nature-based and place-based learning with inspirations from Montessori, Waldorf, and Reggio Emilia principles to create a calm, engaging space for children. As the author of *Overcoming Home Daycare Burnout,* Suzette empowers educators to reclaim their homes and find renewed joy in nurturing young minds.

The neighborhood slowly rises from sleep to the sounds of birdcalls, chirps, and songs. Large and small birds flock to the feeding tree, and a mixture of songs fill the air. The feeding tree attracts the migratory orioles, but this morning robins, chickadees, and sparrows glide through the air. Heard, but not seen, are the calls of the red-winged blackbirds *chaw-chaw*ing atop a tree. The morning sun peeks through the crevices and leaves of the trees, golden glitters flickering like candles in the sky. The hum of vehicles on the distant highway announce the day has begun, and I enjoy the morning walk before our school day begins. Listening to the melodies of birdcalls, chirps, and songs is therapeutic. This natural auditory stress reliever diminishes my anxiety and calms my mind. Undisturbed morning moments are beneficial to my self-care and my ability to work effectively with young children.

For reasons beyond text or research, my welcoming heart prefers to greet the children outdoors each morning, especially when the weather is favorable. Summer warmth in the Midwest affords us longer days of outdoor exploration. And yes, all seasons offer opportunities for outdoor learning, but warmer days allow our play to stretch from drop-off to pickup. Besides, I have found that entering the outdoor space makes a dramatic difference in the children's attitude. Some mornings at indoor drop-off, the children are slow to say goodbye to their families; they linger and cling more, and it becomes a challenge, especially for the emotional child, to separate from the family. But when drop-off happens outdoors, children tend to cheerfully bid their farewell to families

Children with magnetic tiles

as they run off to inquire, wander, and play with their peers. The children's personalities are like nature. I embrace their many unique qualities—their seeds, sprouts, blooms, roots, cracks, flaws, and flares—as they meander into the space they know so well, our little home child care oasis. Our home of outdoor adventures, discoveries, and countless hours of imaginative play.

With lifted spirit and calmness, my body awaits the children's arrival. With my coffee in hand, I tilt my head, enjoying the warmth of the early sun and the crisp morning breeze on my face. In anticipation of spending the morning outdoors, I spread a blanket over a black tarp on the lawn and set out a basket of magnetic tiles. Two of my six children arrive, their faces lighting up when they spot the setup. "Are we going to play outside?" they ask excitedly. Barely waiting for an answer, they hurry to kiss and high-five their parents or caregivers goodbye, then start playing together. Their little voices, cheerful chatter, harmonious play, giggles, and creative collaboration unfold, and happiness envelops me.

I have been a child care provider for sixteen years. It has been a while since I had an African American child in my care, as they seldom come or stay. Yes, I am African American, and my own children have been in my care, but now that they are further along in the school system, I often long for a little person who looks like me.

Childhood Movement and Mysteries

Skip, hop, jump, run, let us dance, pitter-patter rain.
Skip, hop, jump, run, our hands outstretched, let us reach up high.
Skip hop, jump, run, with our knees bent, going low, let us spring up and
reach the sky.
Skip hop, jump, run, let us make more splashes way up so high.
Skip, hop, jump, run, let us prance and splash the sky.

Why do children gather at the window to watch the pitter-patter rain?
I do not know.
Could it be they are waiting to accept the invitation?

Why do children love to play in the rain?
I do not know.
Could it be that the water creates a freedom not contained?

Why do children splash the waters so?
I do not know.
Could it be to learn with science?

Why do children jump in puddles?
I do not know.
Could it be to celebrate their victories?

Children in rainsuits stomping in a puddle

I often think of my childhood days when the rain invited me to play. Days when the water rushing through sidewalk gutters magnetized my feet. Punishments did not deter the soles of my shoes from muddy puddles that beckoned. The absence of wealth kept me happy at the gutter's edge—a place that gave me freedom and delight. It tickled my toes and filled my belly with laughter. Fast-forward forty years, and the natural world that abundantly provided me with rich childhood experiences continues to enrich the young people in my care. I swore I would give them the same experiences I treasured, and I do.

Embracing the Cold Months

In 1998 I immigrated to the United States from Jamaica. I struggled with the winter months, especially those dark, sunless, snowy, cold days, weeks, and months. Illinois is enjoyable in the summer, but winter months are a different story. When I had my first child in 2008, I desperately tried to break the habit of seasonal hibernation. Avoiding the outdoors in winter went contrary to my own childhood and the one I wanted children to have.

In 2009 I opened my home child care, and I was more convinced than ever that all the children would benefit from my love of the outdoors. We enjoyed spring through autumn outside; though winter kept asking for acceptance, we neglected it still. The Midwest was not the tropics, and in my mindset, I saw no possibility of dressing away the cold. On rainy days we rushed outdoors to dance and prance in the puddles. Warm days, our outdoor classroom blossomed with various gardens the children tended, featuring herbs, vegetables, flowers, and fruits as well as visits from butterflies. The backyard was home to all-day lessons in content areas like music, art, and STEM, affording many opportunities for sensory exploration, storytelling, and eating outdoors. Yet during winter, we practically hibernated.

Mindset Shift

In September 2012, a Bulgarian woman came to work with me. She observed how we stayed indoors for weeks. One day she looked at me and insisted, "Miss Sue, the children need to go outside even when it's cold." I hadn't really noticed how often we stayed indoors, which happened whenever the temperature fell to under 60 degrees Fahrenheit.

I heard her, but I was resistant to her appeal. After days of unbiased reflection, I strategically began to find ways to embrace winter. Teachers often transfer our thoughts, feelings, and actions to our students. If we exhibit reluctance toward something, it's not unusual for children to adopt a similar attitude. My son was almost one year old at the time, and my almost three-year-old was not fond of the snow. I have since found ways to help children be comfortable even with the uncomfortable parts of nature and find joy in every season.

My Bulgarian coteacher helped me learn how to dress the children for winter outdoors. She taught me how to bundle them with extra layers of warmth using undergarments, wool socks, hats, scarves, and mittens.

I communicated with families about the change in outdoor activities during the cold months. Some welcomed the transition while others were hesitant, fearing their children would get sick during cold-weather play. We asked families to supply winter garments. Gradually we started to venture outdoors in the cold. Once or twice per week we spent time bundling the children and going outdoors, at times for only ten to twenty minutes of play. The children were not accustomed to cold-weather activities, and although our efforts were often thwarted with cries or children asking to return indoors, we persisted, continuing to make outdoor winter play part of our curriculum and routine.

Having a coteacher meant I could allow some children to stay indoors while the braver ones continued the outdoor adventures. I was the teacher who stayed indoors with the uncomfortable children while my Bulgarian coteacher enjoyed the snow and played with the others. It wasn't long before we increased the time children spent outdoors in the snow. Children were enjoying themselves, lying in the snow to make snow angels, tossing snow, and building snowmen. Gazing out the window, I realized I wanted to be outdoors too—and so did the onlooker children. Bundled in layers of clothing that made movement almost impossible, we waddled outside to join the outdoor group. Have you ever seen a child trying to hold a cup or spoon while wearing mittens? It can be quite challenging! Yet each day we were eager to try going outdoors again, even though getting out with young children requires considerable preparation, with at least thirty minutes of potty and dress time.

By December that year all the children were having a jolly good time loving outdoor winter play. Making snow angels became a reward. It wasn't long before we had our winter break with hopes of starting the new year with many more outdoor play and learning experiences. The Saturday before our school began, I got a call from my coteacher saying she would not return. Disappointed, shocked, and defeated, I committed to making outdoors part of our curriculum even if I was doing it solo. She left us with a new chapter and a joyful way of integrating winter outdoors.

With the departure of my coteacher, I had to find ways to safely work outdoors by myself with mixed-age young children, including infants. This was a challenge for me, as I learned that mud pies aren't only for summer and frozen mud pies are just as fun. Gradually, I came to appreciate the diverse gifts of all seasons and their unique opportunities for teaching. Knowing that some families were hesitant or concerned that their children might fall ill from being outdoors on very cold days, while others didn't equip their children with appropriate outdoor gear, I had to learn how to communicate to the families the profound benefits of outdoor play in all kinds of weather, including when it was hot, raining, or snowing.

I adjusted my handbook, adding pertinent information about outdoor play and learning. Importantly, my new and improved handbook stipulated that families would be required to provide weather-appropriate clothing, including

Snow angel child

warm layers, extra socks, and all-in-one snowsuits that prevent snow from slipping under the jacket. Shopping at the thrift store, I was able to gather extra clothing to ensure all children had appropriate gear for outdoors, even when parents forgot to bring it or perhaps were not able to purchase the gear. Many educators, like myself, implement practical solutions on the fly, such as shopping at a thrift store to ensure all children have the appropriate gear for outdoor play.

I strongly advise fellow educators to communicate the benefits of outdoor learning in all seasons. Drawing upon their own childhood memories of playing outdoors—jumping in mud puddles or rolling in snow—can vividly illustrate these points. Sharing our personal experiences can help families and fellow educators feel more connected and understood in their journey to promote outdoor play. For families who have never experienced such joys, I recommend sharing research-based articles detailing the advantages of outdoor play in children's health and development.

Not many African American families choose my child care. I've been publicly criticized as being too White in culture, though my Caribbean nature-loving ways are rooted in outdoor barefoot play. None of the six African American families who've been enrolled in my child care stayed beyond one year. I recall that one parent asked me not to let their children play in dirt or touch worms, insects, or frogs. She warned against fungus from dirt and salmonella from frogs. I listened and validated her concerns, as my Jamaican culture knows hookworms, roundworms, and parasites so well. However, I asserted to her, there is not enough evidence to prove there are parasites in our backyard soil in the United States. I pointed out how other ground insects, like centipedes, earthworms, earwigs, pill bugs, grubs, slugs, and millipedes, all help the garden.

After effectively communicating the benefits of children exploring nature, explaining how microbes in the dirt help children's immunity, and demonstrating that children live in a world that is not devoid of insects and animals, families began to trust my judgment. In fact, the same client who was apprehensive of her children playing with frogs was relieved when I showed her our makeshift hand-washing station, consisting of a laundry soap container filled with water, hand-washing soap, tea tree oil, and a little vinegar. That natural solution helps clean hands after children handle the spring toads that frequent our yard.

The Seasons

As adults, we too often lose our appreciation for the outdoors, perhaps feeling our lives are too busy to take the time. Or perhaps we were not afforded the opportunity to develop an appreciation for nature due to our families' circumstances. For this reason, it became my mission to help families understand the benefits of outdoor learning and provide children with the opportunity to engage with nature while in my care. Children have an innate way of helping us slow down enough to observe the outdoors in different seasons if we introduce nature play to them at an early age.

Monarch Butterfly

When the spring thaw is on its way and the earth starts *giving*, we welcome birds from far away. Spring flowers poke through the thawed ground and let us know warmer days are on the way. When the songbirds sing early morning tunes, we wake up feeling happy or blue. Migratory birds announce their arrival. Rainy days chase the worms from their burrows and many birds happily glut themselves on the feast. That's when we know it is time to plant seeds.

During the warm summer months, our explorations take us to forest preserves and various nature pathways. However, during COVID, our adventures were confined closer to home. This allowed us to circle our neighborhood more often, finding joy and learning in simple adventures, especially in the dandelion field nearby. In the springtime, the dandelion field is covered with yellow flowers and soon "wish puffs." The field also gives us red clover, turtles, frogs, red-winged blackbirds, praying mantises, grasshoppers, butterflies, and moths. During our walk to the field, we usually look for moss, mushrooms, and squirrel holes in the trees. One day on our walk we stumbled upon white eggs

Children's hands on a sunflower

nestled at the base of a tree. The eggs were larger than a songbird's but smaller than a duck's, with no visible cracks or discoloration. The sight of the unknown eggs sparked a lot of curiosity and guessing among the children. "I bet it's the bunny's," one child confidently declared. "No, it must be a duck's," countered another. Eyes wide with excitement, another child rebutted, "Remember the big bird we saw yesterday? Those must be its eggs!"

Convinced they were dealing with some mysterious bird, the children's curiosity heightened. Each day, they would rush to that spot, hoping to glimpse the mysterious animal sitting on the eggs. For many days, we kept revisiting the place, until one day, the eggs were gone. The disappearance of the eggs catapulted new speculations. "Remember the fox that scared us the other day? He ate the eggs!" said one child. We had entered our backyard and caught sight of the fluffy-tailed creature sleeping in the high grass by the fence. As soon as the creature heard the children's hurried footsteps, it had jumped the fence. On another occasion, we spotted what could have been the same fox with a squirrel in its mouth, and there began a lesson on predators and prey.

Harvesting from the garden

Our backyard transforms into a colorful site of exploration and growth during the summer months. We are gardeners and spend much of our time outdoors. To transform our outdoor classroom, we plant a variety of seeds that the children nurture to maturity. Within our small backyard is a butterfly garden that welcomes monarch, swallowtail, and painted lady butterflies. Adjacent to the butterfly garden is a flower bed with many flowers that feed our pollinators and hummingbirds. The garden also supplies flowers for the children's mud kitchen play. Their little hands take care of their environment, and in turn, the children benefit from the stewardship of their space.

Children harvesting tomatoes from the garden

Summer months allow the children to witness the metamorphosis of caterpillars to butterflies. The monarchs make their way from Mexico and often find our backyard. Each year the first sighting of monarchs happens around June when the host milkweeds are growing and ready to welcome the eggs of the butterflies. I scour the yard to find the eggs and then place them in containers. I do this because I feel that the monarch caterpillars have a higher chance of surviving when we raise them in containers. The children help find eggs or caterpillars on the leaves of the milkweed host plants. They also help to cut young leaves or soft branches to feed the caterpillars. Caterpillars we find can be raised in large fish tanks or standard large butterfly pop-up tents (found online). The children help in this process, and they watch as the caterpillars grow from the size of a tiny inchworm into large, fat caterpillars with ravenous appetites.

Caterpillars eat a lot; therefore, they require a lot of food. The children often watch the caterpillars eat leaves. They have been fortunate to watch them pop out of the chrysalises. In addition, every child in my care has held a butterfly and released one back into nature. We've tagged the end-of-season monarchs that make their way back to Mexico, and each spring we hope to see the ones we tagged return to our backyard. We haven't had such fortune to see a tagged butterfly return to us, but one day we will. Our small backyard garden has made contributions to the miracle of a butterfly voyaging thousands of miles and returning to start the cycle of life again for the next generation—it's a yard that keeps giving.

Another aspect of the garden is the flowers that feed the insects, including butterflies. Sunflower plants, a favorite of ours, are known for their fast growth and congeniality—they smile at the children while chasing the sun. Like guards on duty, the children care for the sunflowers dearly. These sunflowers become a nurturing project. The children water, weed, and guard them diligently against the local wildlife. Despite our efforts, birds and squirrels often find their way to these seeds, sparking a cycle of nature life right before our eyes: squirrels feast on the sunflower seeds, and as the children often tell me, "The foxes eat the squirrels." Though we get frustrated and easily angry with the pesky squirrels

Children among the flowers

during the summer, we compassionately care for them in the cold winter months and often leave apples and other fruits for them—a contradiction the children talk about even years after. Many of their favorite stories begin with, "Remember when the squirrel . . ." Each summer has its garden challenges, and this summer is no different, but we managed to pick some of the flowers before the squirrels got to them.

Then comes Autumn.
The children are tickled by the wind.
Playing with the morning dew.
Crisp morning play, wet grass filled with shiny beads of morning dew.
Walking on grass, getting their shoes wet.
Taking off their shoes, getting their feet wet,
Stomping on the black tarp, making tracks,
Inviting friends to stomp, stomp their feet.
"Look! My footprints are bigger than yours!"
And as time passes, the footprints disappear—
"What happened to the footprints?"
Looking over on the grass, they see the water beads disappear.
"Now we must get spray bottles to wet our feet."
Next morning, I anxiously await the morning dew
in anticipation of giggles and laughter
from children making wet foot tracks.

Children looking up for a bird

Some days the beauty of the day begs our departure to the forest.
And when we venture into the forest, nature's color palette is on full display.
The children's boots hurriedly crunch dried leaves on the yellow path.
One day the noises of our backyard follow us to the forest.
A familiar sound captures the children's attention—
the sharp squawks of blue jays pierce the air.
They stop, look around, then up into the trees—
"Look over there! See it?" one child points excitedly.
"The blue one?" another responds.
"Yes, I see it, I see it!"
"Me too. I see the blue beak."
"No, not the blue beak—the blue feather."
"Oh, yeah, the blue feather."
On this day, the forest truly sings.
Birds soar overhead, and the children play games,
trying to spot the feathery wings in flight.

Autumn's wind, chill, and decay invite winter in. Winter enters our backyard and brings with it changing scenes, sounds, and stillness. It arouses our senses in unique ways. Not many birds or insects are seen or heard, as the children look for other untold mysteries. More than Popsicle cold, they feel the sting of winter in their fingers and toes—it's been years since I feared winter, but many children still do not like to wear gloves or mittens. Winter holds space for learning and observations—from the daggerlike icicles dangling from the roof's edge to the foggy puffs of our breath in the frosty air.

We care for the cold creatures that visit our patio, watching for birds that stay for the season. The bird feeder becomes a bustling hub for the elusive junco, seen only in the chill, and the vibrant cardinals, sparrows, and woodpeckers, while the robins take their leave until warmer days return. These moments teach children about the resilience of nature.

Walking on winter's snowy, icy grounds, the children develop their gross-motor skills in ways the other seasons cannot offer. Each slip and fall is a lesson in balance and movement—teaching them where to step and how intensely or widely they need to move and stride. Winter isn't always gray as some may say: winter is silver, golden, bronze, and white, it is metallic, and it shimmers with the sun. Winter creates ice play instead of mud. Our outdoor kitchen remains open, ready for the children to break ice, make snow cupcakes, and stir until the thaw comes. With each passing year, winter opens our doors to new cold adventurous days. And with each winter, I get braver and demand more hours outdoors, yes, more hours of outdoor play.

Conclusion

For any educator facing skepticism about the value of outdoor learning, seek the counsel of those who have navigated this path before. Draw on the insights and experiences of fellow educators who have adapted their practices to support children's engagement with nature. Cultures vary, and while some caregivers may initially resist outdoor activities, it's helpful to encourage families to reflect on their own childhood interactions with nature and deeply consider what the modern world may be denying their children.

Nature provides us with its cycles: Seeds sprout into flowers, fruits, and vegetables; large trees offer shade that makes us grateful on sweltering days and offer sanctuary for diverse wildlife. All children deserve to experience the call of the wild—hills, streams, valleys, prairie lands, woodlands, and meadows. These natural spaces soothe their emotions and envelop them in a blanket of sensory experiences and learning.

Children at a picnic

Our enclosed backyard has become a classroom under the sky, where the children learn about nature and partake in many meals outdoors. This connection with nature is not just educational; it nurtures their bodies, minds, and spirits, providing a holistic growth environment that indoor settings seldom offer.

Mud play

Reflection Questions

1. Think about your personal connection to nature. Were you allowed to play outdoors? Why or why not? What stories did your parents, grandparents, great-grandparents, or society tell about your culture and the outdoors?

2. What barriers are preventing you from integrating nature into your classroom? Was it taboo for you to be outdoors as a child? Is it taboo for the children you care for?

3. Consider how your environment can support children's learning and exploration. Look around your yard and ask yourself what skills children can learn within your gates. If your childhood didn't include outdoor play, ask yourself what you can add to the environment to fulfill your own childhood dreams.

4. Do you need a lot of space for experiences in nature, or can integrating a small section of outdoor space make a big impact? Think about simple solutions; for example, can a small blanket help children delight in eating outdoors if you don't have a table? How much help will you need to provide a nature space for children to explore? Who in your community and networks can provide this support?

CHAPTER 12

The Outdoor Neighborhood Classroom

Jasmin Field, Edgewood, MD

Jasmin Field earned a degree in theater arts from Michigan State University and acted professionally in Washington, DC, while working as an activities leader at an Alzheimer's care facility. Her passion for teaching was ignited during her service with AmeriCorps, as she helped improve child literacy in Baltimore, Maryland. As a lead pre-K teacher at the Goddard School of Bel Air, she developed various teaching methods that later inspired her innovative homeschooling approach during the pandemic. In 2021 she earned her Nature-Based Learning Certification from the Association for Nature-Based Education (ANBE) (formerly ERAFANS) and launched the Edgewood Outdoor Neighborhood Classroom in her yard in Edgewood, Maryland, creating memorable educational experiences for children through more than seventy-five outdoor activities.

Sometimes outsiders immediately want to write off a neighborhood. A shooting, mugging, or robbery makes the newspaper (more than once), and onlookers outside the community begin making negative assumptions about the next generation and its prospects for contributing to society. News coverage of crimes can sometimes reflect bias, including negative portrayals of communities of color. Studies have shown that people of color, particularly Black and Latino individuals, are often overrepresented as suspects or perpetrators in crime stories, while White individuals may be portrayed in more sympathetic or neutral ways, even when involved in similar incidents (Callanan 2012). Even though studies have shown that newspaper reports on crime and violence in communities of color are biased, the negative perception still persists. Yet, an *insider* perspective highlights the inspirational stories in between those biased headlines.

In July 2023, at the opening session of my outdoor classroom in our yard, I took a moment to look into the eyes of the eager students under my tent. "Do you all know that Edgewood has a reputation? Do you all know that *you* have a reputation just because you live in Edgewood?" Genuine expressions of ignorance looked back at me. "No," they said, shaking their heads and shrugging.

I took a breath and answered back, "Well, it does, and it's not the best one. Lots of bad things happen here, but what we want to show the community is that those aren't the *only* things that go on here. We want to make sure people know there are kids in Edgewood who want to do right, who care about education and want to explore the wonders of nature. Let's make sure we challenge our reputation just by showing up here, having fun, and learning together this summer." Everyone nodded their heads in agreement, and I smiled as we launched into our schedule of outdoor adventures in my backyard.

The Vision

Child potential has always had a loud voice in our part of the neighborhood. Our street is filled with active children who are excited to pursue adventures, friendships, and new experiences. This eagerness to learn really started showing itself when in the spring of 2023 I began bringing my family's homeschool activities outdoors, including sensory tables, natural items, and project tools. My own children were four years old and two years old, which drew the attention of many pre-K-aged children on our street. The homes in our neighborhood do not include garages, but instead we share a parking lot in the center of our street. This makes it easy to watch one another, whether a person peers through a window or observes neighbors from their front porch. Children returning home from school and child care were ready to engage in activities that didn't station them at desks, and they became intrigued at the sight of our family as we brought out tables and other materials in preparation for outdoor learning. They flooded over to us in groups, eagerly asking if they could participate. We were starting our pursuit of earth crafts and dirt interactions. Taking a break from bike rides and balls, they thoroughly enjoyed incorporating dirt and leaves into our sensory experience, as well as digging their hands into the kinetic sand. They loved that the purpose of the activity was getting dirty! Limited by a short recess at school, they were glad to explore freely outside in this way once they returned home.

Later on in the spring, my husband, Justin, a middle school math teacher, heard about the children's responses and wanted to see how they would do in an area of his strength: a math activity. Once he brought out writing utensils, a group of children gathered on our front lawn. Clearly, they were ready to get to work, as they quickly solved the equations he gave them.

I felt encouraged as even more children asked if they could join in. Soon our Field family activities were becoming an exciting time in our neighborhood, as local children of all ages felt welcome to join in our learning. As the weather warmed, it invited even more activities, and I was encouraged by the children's anticipation.

Though our front porch was large enough to house pencils, notebooks, and other learning tools, only a handful of children could sit together in such a small space. When I became aware of the large number of children who wanted to be a part of our activities, we began using the sidewalk in front of our home as a base to write answers, create pictures, and play games. These open spaces in front of our home were enough for a casual lesson or two, but we often extended into the parking lot when we wanted to do separate group activities or give the kids their own creation space.

As our outdoor classroom continued to spill out into the neighborhood, we realized that even if our neighbors had tolerated our activities up to a point, it was likely some would object to chalk designs in front of their homes and projects being built next to their cars on a regular basis. We wanted to provide a bigger space that we could personalize and design for the children's enjoyment and learning needs. Our open, fenceless backyard was the most available option and seemed like a great fit since it was our own property and we had the freedom to share it. Located at the end of a connected unit of homes, it was bigger than most other yards on our street and was very visible to nearby parents through their home windows.

A view of a potential classroom space in our yard

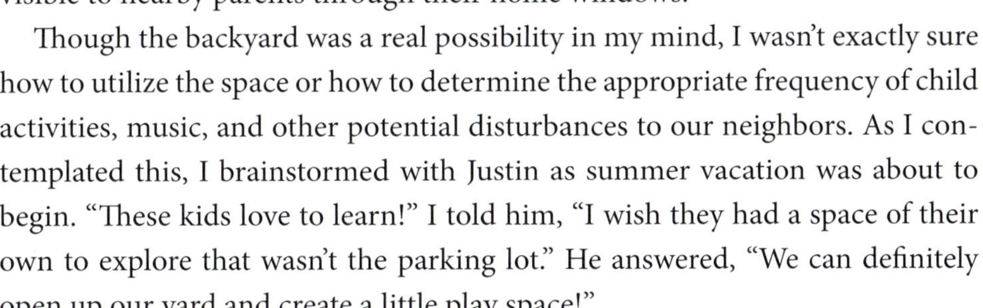

Though the backyard was a real possibility in my mind, I wasn't exactly sure how to utilize the space or how to determine the appropriate frequency of child activities, music, and other potential disturbances to our neighbors. As I contemplated this, I brainstormed with Justin as summer vacation was about to begin. "These kids love to learn!" I told him, "I wish they had a space of their own to explore that wasn't the parking lot." He answered, "We can definitely open up our yard and create a little play space!"

As I thought about the kind of space I wanted to provide, I hoped to make an experience more exciting than climbing domes and kiddie pools. I knew I had more to offer the children in my neighborhood if I was willing to challenge myself, think outside the box, and take some risks. I completed the Association for Nature-Based Education (ANBE) Outdoor Education certification program in September 2021, and I recognized this as a great opportunity to share what I had learned. Although I had felt a personal and spiritual connection to the outdoors since high school, I hadn't yet explored ways to incorporate this interest into my teaching. I knew prior to having children that I was interested in some sort of further education, but I wanted it to be unique and a true reflection of my interests.

While browsing outdoor activities to pursue with my two children, I was grateful to come across the ANBE certification program and was immediately fascinated by the direct interaction with the earth the program encouraged and the evident benefits children received when they focused on relationships with people and the earth around them. Learning this method of teaching was stimulating, hands-on, and creative. After I completed the program, I was excited to introduce more nature-based learning opportunities to my own children and loved watching their responses to entomology, land and water exploration, and previously indoor activities I restructured to take outside. I didn't realize it at the time, but this was the birth of my vision to share these learning experiences with children in our neighborhood that came to fruition the next year.

It wasn't until I witnessed an increase in parking lot play time—and parking lot boredom—at the beginning of summer break in 2023 that I began to understand the unique chance I had to provide a more enriching summer to these children. The real question was whether I was willing to commit my time and energy. I knew from their responses to us that the children in our neighborhood were available and willing to participate in any activity we offered, but what I ultimately decided is that they didn't need "more of the same." They were ready to be challenged, to learn in new ways and readjust their perspectives on what was already around them. Thinking beyond the traditional classroom was sure to encourage creative and critical thinking in fresh ways.

It was from here that the idea of exploring nature within our community began stirring in my brain. We had limitations: modest finances, growing relationships with parents who may or may not have been comfortable with us teaching their children, and a residential backyard space that had to remain within zoning regulations of our city as it related to the number of people in our yard and the types of activities we pursued. Though some of these conditions felt like setbacks, there was a very real freedom we could also embrace to try new things, welcome neighborhood children into the experience, and pay attention to nature in detailed ways we hadn't before. We had freedom to explore the complexities of the trees, birds, dirt, insects, and plants all around us! We pressed into that freedom and decided to take the risk by sending invites to all the families on our street with young children, giving them a general description of class activities we had planned.

The Launch

We knocked on doors to invite neighborhood children, rang our cowbell in the center of our backyard each afternoon when class was about to begin, and set up table stations incorporating art, food science, and gardening around the yard.

Though it began as an "open" exploration experience, I realized early on that we needed some form of structure to keep the children focused as we were using one space together in a variety of ways. We asked ourselves: *How can a larger understanding of nature be gained through activities in this one backyard?* We had to meet the children halfway between the school system they had known their whole lives and the "looseness" of letting the journey of exploration lead them. Ongoing reflection helped us to reorganize our program and

Nature kitchen and food science station with fun facts sheet for discussion

find a balance between learning from my husband and me and the children's own self-guided learning. We decided on a regular format of introducing daily fun facts and providing the tools the children needed to make these fun facts interactive. For example, during our week focused on rocks and mountains, our nature kitchen featured a box of large rocks and bowls of Cheerios. After learning that rocks were one of the earliest kitchen tools used to crush grain thousands of years ago, all the children were excited to pick up rocks and crush some of their own! "Ground Cheerio powder" became a favorite activity that helped them to connect history, food science, and the use of earth tools. Each session, we split our class time between goal-based projects at each station in the yard (similar to the aforementioned activity), followed by children's choice activities, a time when they could repeat an activity they enjoyed or explore freely with provided tools at each station.

Jasmin Field's food science during The Wonder of Water week (*Baltimore Sun* photo)

It was incredibly encouraging to watch parents I hardly knew bring over lawn chairs, see how we learned together, and then offer to assist with snack distribution at the end of each class as we discussed our favorite moments for the day. I felt blessed to feel trusted when a mom of seven sent her children over together, peeking from the window of their home every once in a while to see their smiles and focused faces. It wasn't until an article was written about our project in the *Baltimore Sun* in July 2023 that I got to hear parent feedback that I will always carry with me. One parent was quoted in the article as saying, "Every day, they come in here and tell me about nature stuff, and she teaches them about the Bible. They just adore it all." This article was a community victory. The children were thrilled to knock on all the neighbors' doors to share the news. We were thankful that our neighbors supported our project, and we wanted them to know that this article was a celebration not just for the participants but for all of us in Edgewood! What an honor to be a part of a positive publication that highlighted youth potential, education, and purpose in learning.

This is where the love for this program started and still continues. I've had a growing realization that God loves the children in this neighborhood and wants each child to connect with Him through the earth—the same earth that their ancestors utilized, explored, and learned from. Doing this work is an absolute privilege, and I smile with all that's inside of me when I watch these children make their city—the city that many don't pay any mind—shine so bright.

Even as I watched the children smile and engage, a part of me wasn't certain that what we were learning in the backyard was being retained beyond the day's lesson. I'll never forget that after the conclusion of our "rocks and mountains" lesson, as I was packing up the yard for the evening, I spotted a group of children walking past with large rocks in their hands. Usually, a tablet was the favored item to bring outside, but this time it looked as though they had chosen a new game. "What is that you're holding?" I yelled out to them as they walked by. Smiling and proud, they yelled back "*rocks!*" As I realized they were on their way to create some form of food grinding station, I was encouraged to see them incorporating a new version of play into their time together. Their learning was resonating with them, and they were having fun as they realized the world around them was available for further exploration.

Lillian with rocks and shapes page

An Encouraged City

As I received emails from article readers, I was supported by Edgewood residents to continue the program and thanked for my efforts to invest in children within the community. Really, I should have been thanking them. I'm thankful that the children go on these journeys of discovery with me as we investigate countless bean types, build a clay Mount Everest while learning the story of a sixteen-year-old girl who climbed it, or discover unknown fun facts about the creatures we commonly interact with in our neighborhood. What an awesome use of a magnifier to observe the five heartbeat patterns of a worm!

Since 2022 our program has grown wonderfully in participation and content. We were able to hold over forty nature-based activities in July 2023 and featured two amazing guest speakers that enhanced our knowledge greatly: a planetary geologist and a naturalist from our local nature center.

Naturalist visit

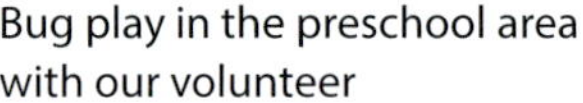

Bug play in the preschool area with our volunteer

Dulaney's tree branch art

The amount of support we received from parents, children, local church volunteers, and surrounding nature programs has left my husband and me speechless. We are excited to continue this amazing work of connecting with nature in our little city as the wonder of measuring trees, painting with mud, and engineering tree branch bridges for small critters unites us through teamwork and friendship, creating memories for a lifetime.

I challenge any and every educator to reach back toward the children living in nearby residential areas who may be reaching out to them. It's not easy to commit a portion of your time without fail and continue moving forward when new obstacles are facing you. But it can be life-changing when you are the catalyst for an experience that unites a community for the benefit of children's education.

Reflecting on my background in professional theater, child literacy, pre-K teaching, and event planning, I recognize how I combined learned skills from each profession to create an inviting and engaging environment for all involved. Each station we created was a miniature stage, inviting children to step into a world of outdoor art, science labs, and more. For teachers, setting the stage of a classroom is a key component in creating an approachable, inviting, and energized environment to learn. I was excited to create a little nature world in our backyard each day, encouraged that we would share our favorite moments under tents, below tree branches, and on our tree stump stage area.

I'm not a nature guru, but I'm drawn to the whispers of the wind and rustling of the river. I took that passion and created a way for people, both young and old, to interact with one another and the natural world. I did my best to make what I valued personal, educational, and approachable. I'm forever grateful when I unlock the door to my home and hear a voice behind me yell, "Is it almost time for the next outdoor classroom?" I encourage anyone who doubts what they can accomplish to take a risk and be proud of whatever it becomes.

Think about your passions and your skills. How can you share them with others who are hungry to learn? It begins with your willingness to invite in the people around you. Even if all you have to offer is a small fraction of your day or week, your commitment and consistency convey that they are valued. Think of how you might use one of your skills to help build a child's character, inspire a vision for their future, and teach them how to remain committed to something important to them. Learning takes many forms, and the classroom can take the form of your own backyard, with a foldable table brought out once a week as the workspace. Invest in yourself as a growing person by helping others grow around you. When a child has a guide who exposes them to something bigger, it can be the beginning of a great adventure for both the student and the teacher.

Reflection Questions

1. What is a passion of yours that you are always excited to discuss with others? How can that interest, talent, or skill be turned into a tangible activity?
2. What is the reputation of the area you live in? Take note of any neighbors (adults and children) you see at a distance. Consider what it would be like to invest in building a relationship with them, even if just to know the people around you a little better.
3. What elements of character and education do you feel equipped to pass on to the next generation?

References

Callanan, Valerie J. 2012. "Media Consumption, Perceptions of Crime Risk and Fear of Crime: Examining Race/Ethnic Differences." *Sociological Perspectives* 55 (1): https://doi.org/10.1525/sop.2012.55.1.93.

SECTION IV

Inquiry Through Nature

NATURE AND INQUIRY go hand in hand. The limitless explorations, the questions that come from seeing things, change moment to moment. Here, again, is that impermanence of nature that lends itself to the wonder we feel for nature and where Spanish provides us with language that comes close to describing the eternal and temporal aspects of nature. *Los amaneceres son hermosos y el de hoy está asombroso*, sunrises are beautiful and the one today is amazing. The fleeting essence of nature creates a setting in which children's curiosities become the driving force for learning, with the potential to culminate in experiences that last a year or longer, even as nature shifts moment to moment.

The process of inquiry is cyclical, with students driving the learning and teachers providing the experiences that give students fodder to keep wondering, questioning, gathering information, making predictions, analyzing, exploring, and discussing. They build collective knowledge. One question leads to another, which leads to a prediction that leads to an experiment that leads to more questions. In essence, it's the process of scientific learning. One day a house finch appears in the schoolyard, and then the next day there are two house finches, one more brightly colored than the other. Then, a few days later, the children notice finches in the overhang of the school building carrying twigs in their beaks. Every day, something new happens. All these happenings lead to more and more curiosity and questions. The same cannot be said for the static magnetic tiles and wooden blocks in the classroom.

In section 4 you will encounter examples of how educators lean into the kinship and relationship we have with the natural world. These are examples of how nature lends itself to profound learning that impacts not only the students and teachers but also spills over in its bounty to the families and community. My story recounts how digging up worms in our local park made the humble worm into an integral part of each child's family. Flor Villanueva-Winter shares how her students adopted a tree—and then brought Max inside their classroom.

Reflection Questions

1. How can educators foster a learning environment in which students' curiosity about the ever-changing natural world becomes the driving force for inquiry, and how can language—such as the Spanish phrases that express the beauty and impermanence of nature—enhance their understanding and connection to the world around them?
2. In what ways can you connect the vast array of cultural knowledge each child brings into the school day to their learning experiences in nature?
3. What are two easy ways you can start to integrate the cycle of inquiry into your work? In what ways can you support the cyclical process of inquiry, ensuring that students' questions and observations lead to ongoing exploration, collaboration, and scientific discovery?

CHAPTER 13

"The Hearts Are for the Worms!" Family, Home, and Culture Through Worms

Jessica Fong, Chicago, IL

Jessica Fong first taught in a formal classroom in 2007 at a small, multicultural academy in her native Guatemala in a multi-age classroom of first- through third-grade students. She began working full-time as a preschool teacher in 2012 at a private school and transitioned to Chicago Public Schools, where she taught preschool-aged students. She received her master's degree in early childhood education from DePaul University in 2010 and a master's degree in dual-language education at Roosevelt University in 2018. She is currently pursuing a doctorate in educational sustainability at the University of Wisconsin–Stevens Point.

THE LOWLY WORM is never lowly in the eyes of a child. The worm is a sentient being that needs love and care, community, and family. In the 2018–19 school year, I came to see worms through the eyes of my students, even as I saw myself in the children.

I have countless core memories from my childhood of encounters with animals, from cicadas to worms. Every being needed my support, and I took my work seriously. I remember saving drowning worms from puddles, hoping they would come back from the dead even when they were gray and listless. I would lie on the picnic bench in my concrete backyard in Chicago and feed tiny crumbs to the network of ants that marched from crack to crack. Neighbors knew me as the child who took in injured birds and rehabilitated them, helping them get back on their tiny feet with care, food, and water. I would rejoice when it was time to let them go, and then wipe away tears as I watched them return to where they belonged. I remember writing a poem in middle school called "Alone but with the Birds," whose title still runs through my head whenever I birdwatch or hear birds sing. Small birds, wet worms, and tiny ants were the gentle threads that wove the fabric of my childhood together.

As a classroom educator, I took my natural caring to another level by creating spaces for my students to connect to nature in the ways I did as a child. When my students started using sticks to dig in the soil to find worms at our local park, I was ready to delve into the world that had cultivated so much joy in me as a child.

In the fall of 2018, I began working at a Reggio-inspired early childhood center. We focused on one schoolwide theme every year, and that year, the work centered on David Sobel's 2008 book, *Childhood and Nature: Design Principles for Educators*. My classroom was what is called a blended or inclusive classroom as defined by the Chicago Public Schools, consisting of a blend of general education students and students with special needs. We had three educators to support the students: Ms. Erin, the special education teacher, Ms. Sandra, the paraprofessional, and me, the general education teacher. Ms. Erin, Ms. Sandra, and I decided to focus on Animal Allies, one of the themes from Sobel's book, drawing in particular from his statement that "Animals play a significant role in the evolution of children's care about the natural world and in their own emotional development" (29).

And so it was that our work exploring nature began in the fall of 2018, growing naturally out of the children's explorations and discoveries at our local park. McKinley Park is a sixty-nine-acre public park in the heart of the city of Chicago, located just half a block from the school. During the first few weeks of school, we visited the park and invited the children to explore. In our initial trips, all the children showed an interest in digging, and as they dug, they began to find earthworms. Digging for earthworms became a favorite pastime, and the children began bringing the earthworms back to the classroom, which we happily facilitated by using an empty fish tank to recreate the earthworms' natural habitat. We had begun incorporating the worms into our classroom, doing what Sobel (2008) describes as "weav[ing] the clans together" (30); that is, children were beginning to see nature as part of their larger family, or kin. The worms became part of their daily lives, and in turn the worms also became part of the children's families.

Early on, the children began to identify with the earthworms and give them humanlike properties such as genders, emotions, and families. Children showed a deep understanding of how to care for a living creature and how they experience being cared for in their own lives. Here and below, the children's names are pseudonyms.

Sara: Look it. It's so cute.

Eduardo: It's so cute. Look at my hand. Oh my goodness! He likes that. (Eduardo uses a finger to gently touch the worm in his other hand.)

Eduardo: Hey, I wanna touch the worm. Whoa, he's doing tricks.

Sara: She's dirty on herself. Yeah, she's dirty.

Eduardo: Lookit what he's doing on my hand.

Sara: Lookit, she's so super. She's gotta wash her hair. Lookit, she's so cute.

Eduardo: He's still tired, look. Because he wanna go his mom.

Sara: She's so dirty.

Eduardo: Look what he's doing in my hand. Maybe he's trying to get out. He's spinning.

In the early days of the study, we provided children with paper and black permanent markers to draw what they observed about the worms. Pretty quickly, the children decided to put the earthworms they brought from the park directly onto the paper they were drawing on and drew items for the worms. The worms' bodies also left yellow stains as they wiggled around. One student, Ebel, exclaimed, "It's yellow because it's going to pee. Maybe he's trying to find Mommy. It's lying down. He met his mom. He's slippery. I'm going to make a home." He then used a black marker to draw a circle around the worm on the paper.

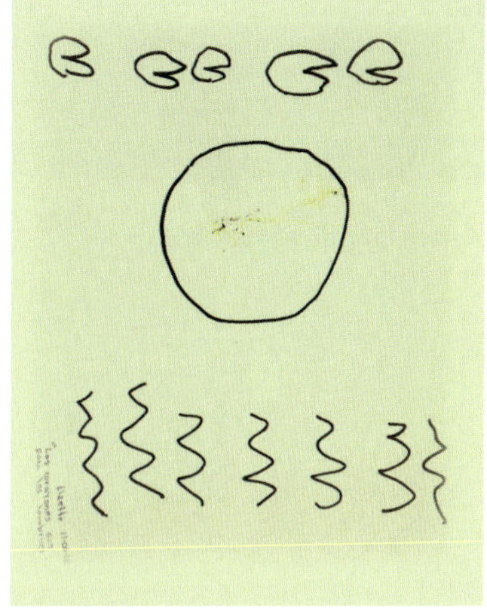
Lily's drawing

Lily's drawing included a home for the worm, as shown by the center circle around the worms that were on the paper. Lily also added hearts and said, "*Los corazones son para la lombriz* (The hearts are for the worms)." Other children's drawings included food for the worms as well as additional worm family members. Aria's drawing shows lines at the bottom of the drawing with the longer lines being mama and papa and the shorter lines being her brother, her best friend, and herself. At the top of the drawing is the sun with an apple and banana for food for the worm family. The children's understanding of what worms eat came from their experiments with Ms. Sandra.

Ms. Sandra brought to this study her love of composting using red wiggler worms. For years, Ms. Sandra had a compost bin in her classroom and brought it out occasionally to show the children how she fed the red wigglers. Red wiggler worms, or *Eisenia fetida,* are an excellent species for breaking down organic material, which is why they are used for vermicomposting and are sold for this purpose. The earthworms, or *Lumbricus terrestris,* that the children brought back to school from the park are best known for their soil aeration. Because we had access to plentiful red wiggler worms in Ms. Sandra's bin, she conducted an experiment with the students to see what the red wiggler worms would eat. The children helped Ms. Sandra place apples, oranges, and bananas in the worm bin and returned to the bin each week to see what the worms had eaten. These food items became part of the children's stories, drawings, and paintings.

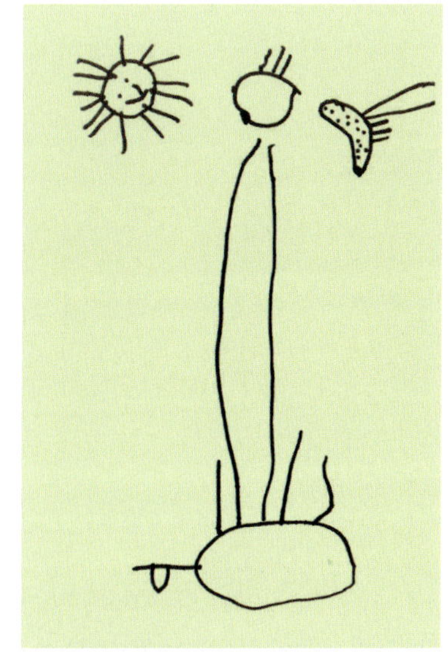
Aria's drawing

This deep care for the worms in general became an interest in caring for their own individual red wiggler worm, which we supplied for each child. Each child selected their worm, named it, created a small home for it, and took it home. While keeping undomesticated animals as pets is generally frowned upon in the world of conservation, the red wiggler worms we sent home are prolific and we strongly believed in the benefit to the children engaging with the worms in this way.

The small homes all started from the same base, clear food containers we had collected. Each child added the soil and food items they felt their worm would want. The final touch was their worm's name written with black permanent marker on a colorful strip of tape. We provided the families with simple

Anabel hugging her worm

written instructions on how to care for the worms and sent home small droppers for putting water in the worm homes. We also put a few "extra" worms in the small containers to ensure success. We let the caregivers know that the children had been helping take care of the worms in the classroom, so they had knowledge of how to do it, and each child also took home a small blank booklet to write the story of their worm's time at home.

Anabel and Darla both showed a deep love for their pet worms. Anabel and her family created a panel of photos with Anabel's words about her pet worm, Mr. Boy, that she shared with her classmates. When it was Darla's turn to share her worm Andy's story with her classmates, she hopped from one leg to the other while twirling around throughout her presentation, holding her worm's home in one hand. While sharing the story she and her family wrote about Andy, she exclaimed, "This is the words for my beautiful pet!"

While not every family was excited at first to receive a pet worm at home, every single family supported their children's explorations. One family member in particular, Abel's mother, had a deep disgust for the worms, but she was deeply motivated to share her son's joy for his worm. Our family exploration activity, where we invited families into the school to participate alongside their children in the worm study, was the perfect opportunity for her to share in the joy with her son.

The activity in the spring was a culminating experience for the children and their families to explore the materials the children had used throughout the school year—clay, acrylic paint, and black permanent markers with an overlay of watercolor paint—and to coconstruct portraits of their child's worm. We provided all families with multiple entry points using the materials to engage

Darla dancing. Darla can be seen as a blur as she twirls and dances while presenting about her worm, Andy.

Left: Abel and his mom

Right: Anabel's grandmother guides Anabel in manipulating the clay by saying, "*Hazlo así, mija. Así como cuando hacemos tortillas.*" (Do it like this, my child. Like when we make tortillas).

with the worms. We had tools for clay, gloves, multiple-sized permanent markers, and different-sized paintbrushes. Although these tools are traditionally used for specific materials—paintbrushes for paint and clay tools for clay—we offered the flexibility to use them in whatever way suited each individual. We also did this with the students throughout the study. One of the hallmarks of an inquiry-based classroom is to provide a variety of tools and materials for children to use to construct and explore their understandings of the topics at hand.

It was this flexible approach with materials and tools that provided Abel's mother with an entry into engaging with the worms. She used the end of a paintbrush to interact with the worms, rather than her bare hands. The fact that she engaged with the worms at all showed a shift in her attitude from disgust to curiosity. It was a shift we saw over and over in both the children and the adults and a shift that drove the curiosity momentum in the classroom.

The family exploration was one of the richest that we had as educators through the two years we worked with these children. We connected what the children were experiencing at home and at school and saw the profound impact caring for such small creatures had for the children as well as their families.

Our work with children with special needs also sparked moments of deep reflection and learning for us as educators. Two children in particular, Gina and Darla, affected our work not only with them but with all the children in the classroom. In the beginning of the study, when the children were digging for worms and picking them up, Gina had a deep aversion to the sensation of worms touching her hands. Throughout most of the year, she would stand on the side next to groups of students who were looking for earthworms outside, watching and observing. As the other children began to engage with the worms

Darla's worm home drawing

Collaborative worm portraits

by holding them, she would scream that she wanted to hold a worm as her classmates were doing, but when one of us put one on her hand, she would scream and drop it immediately. We were not sure what to do with Gina's reaction and could not figure out how to help her. It was clear she desperately wanted to hold a worm, but she couldn't stand to keep it in her palm. Ms. Erin thought one day to give her a pair of gloves. She thought perhaps the sensorial experience of having a wet, wiggling worm on her palm was too much for Gina. Ms. Erin carefully helped Gina put on a pair of blue medical gloves. The gloves were much too large for her small hands, yet they were enough. We gently placed a plump worm in her outstretched palms. Gina looked down and realized she could finally hold a worm. Although she remained a little wary of the worm in this initial encounter, gingerly poking at it with one gloved finger, within a few days she was happily interacting with the worms using the gloves.

Darla communicated her theories about worms and their homes through richly detailed drawings. Darla came to our classroom choosing not to speak to teachers or peers while in school, although her mother shared that at home Darla was very talkative. Yet she was a passionate and active participant in our worm study from the onset. Because we provided multiple points of entry into the exploration of worms outside of verbal communication, Darla was able to be an active participant in the exploration. By providing students with the opportunity not only to talk about their worms but also to draw them, touch them, and feed them, every child could engage in the excitement.

One day Ms. Erin asked Darla the name of her worm and Darla drew a picture of a rectangle and then quietly, but not audibly, said the name. Ms. Erin was excited to hear Darla's words but did not initially understand her, even after a few attempts. Neither Darla nor Ms. Erin gave up. They stayed together for nearly thirty minutes as Darla attempted to say the word, draw the word, and pantomime the word to be understood. Darla even chose to forgo gross-motor play in the gym to continue trying to communicate the name of her worm. Finally, Ms. Erin thought of calling Darla's mother, who took a moment out of her workday to help her daughter be understood. Darla's mother knew immediately what Ms. Erin was talking about when describing her daughter's drawing. Pillow Elsa! The worm's name was Pillow Elsa and her daughter's name was Ana. After that day, Darla began to carefully choose words to verbally communicate with her classmates and teachers.

We often assume as educators that the work we do with students has to be complex and elaborate, mostly because of the standards that are set by school districts and administrators. Yet there are few if any standards set around curiosity and joy, and what is learning if it's not about that? Think about some of your core memories from your early school experiences. Chances are they are not memories of worksheets and memorization. Our worm study showed us how something so small could be so magnificent. Years after this study, we had families let us know that their children still talked about their worms. One even kept his worm alive for at least a year after he left our classroom. These tiny liaisons, or go-betweens, acted as connectors to bridge nature to our student's lives. They fell in love with their worms and imagined their little lives with mommies, daddies, and babies, mirroring their own lives. Through this love, the children learned to care for and about nature. As these young humans were learning who they were outside of their homes and developing their identities through their exposure to the world around them, they had an experience that showed them that every being was just like them in so many ways.

Gina standing on the sidelines

Gina using gloves to handle worms

Thoughts to Guide Similar Work

- **Connect the learning in your classroom to the experiences students and their families have at home.** Children often go home and excitedly share what happened at school that day. It's a much richer experience for the children to be able to connect the two environments that are so important to their development in their early years.
- **Provide multiple points of entry** into the study so all students can engage in the way that feels most comfortable for them.
- **Use multiple materials.** This group of children studied worms through clay, acrylic paint, and permanent markers with a watercolor overlay. Using this rich variety of materials, the children could delve into the world of the animals around them. Each material was introduced over time, purposefully letting children explore the material over many weeks before asking them to create something with the material. This material exploration was integral to the work in helping the children explore their wonderings and understandings of the worms.
- **Story dictation** became a powerful tool in helping my students tell stories about their worms. The child dictates, or tells, their story while the adult writes it down. The child is also invited to draw their story. Then each child may share their story with their peers through dramatization. When this practice becomes frequent in the classroom, the stories become more and more complex, and all children start looking forward to acting out the stories.

Reflection Questions

1. How did this story remind you of your own experiences with animals, and why?
2. How did this chapter influence your perspective on working with children and animals?
3. Why do you think animals have such a profound impact in connecting families to the classroom, and what are some initial steps you can take to integrate animal allies into your students' learning experiences?
4. What would incorporating experiences with animals in your teaching practice look like, both in and out of the classroom?

References

Sobel, David. 2008. *Childhood and Nature: Design Principles for Educators.* Stenhouse Publishers.

CHAPTER 14

Max the Tree

Flor Villanueva-Winter, Chicago, IL

A native of Colombia, Flor Villanueva-Winter is an early childhood educator at Belmont-Cragin Elementary, a dual-language (Spanish and English) Chicago public school. She has been teaching preschoolers following the Reggio approach for more than nineteen years. Flor is a recipient of the Kohl McCormick Early Childhood Teaching Award for her work with developmentally disabled infants and families. She has also conducted seminars for the Chicago Metro Association for the Education of Young Children. She holds a master's degree in early childhood education from the Erikson Institute.

OUR STUDY OF Max the tree is not just a story of a single tree but of all the trees children encounter in their neighborhoods, parks, forest preserves, and more. The study of Max was developed by the preschool students at Belmont-Cragin Elementary, a dual-language (Spanish and English) Chicago public school, as they became interested in learning about trees and nature, guided by me as their lead teacher. Our preschool program is inspired by the Reggio approach. It has seven preschool classrooms in total, five full-day and two half-day. The Belmont-Cragin Elementary School is located on the west side of Chicago and serves a population of students who are 95.5 percent Latino.

This particular study of Max the tree began during October 2021, when the trees started to feel the wind blowing here and there and the leaves were changing colors. It was the beginning of the fall season.

The Philosophy of Education

The teacher's mission in early childhood is to be reflective, an interpreter of the students' interests and knowledge. Children always express their feelings, thoughts, interests, theories, and wonderings by using many languages in addition to their oral and written language, including kinesthetic, aesthetic, social, and emotional languages. Dr. Loris Malaguzzi, psychologist, educator, and creator of the Reggio approach, introduced the concept of "one hundred languages" to make clear that children have many languages to express their knowledge.

In the Reggio approach, children and teachers learn as they engage in studies that can sometimes span an entire school year. The studies are guided by provocations, or experiences designed by the educators to spark curiosity, and they follow cycles of inquiry that lead the children and educators deeper and deeper into the topic. While the topics and materials that children and teacher explore are varied, nature and the outdoors can provide endless possibilities and ever-changing phenomena that are fertile grounds for a year-long study.

We teachers attentively observe students' processes of learning when they construct their own knowledge by expressing and representing their feelings, thoughts, interests, theories, and wonderings in many ways, using the language(s) with which they feel confident and secure: children's words, drawings, sculptures, actions, and so on.

Another role of the teacher is to help the students in connecting their knowledge and making sense of their own meanings and wonderings. This intellectual activity goes in two directions: teachers to students and students to teachers. Both are together in this process of analyzing, reflecting, and making meaning of the students' representations and verbal expressions, sometimes expressed in metaphors. Teachers also develop their own conclusions. A class conversation about the students' opinions and expressions, through drawings, paintings, three-dimensional artifacts, or verbal expressions such as metaphors, dialogues, and comments, should be done on a regular basis in a Reggio-inspired classroom. We start our mornings with large group conversations and chanting. Large and small group conversations provide an important space for the class to engage in reflections and analysis about their discoveries through dialogues, questions, answers, and making connections. Teachers and students participate at an equal level of learning, with everyone becoming researchers in discovering and experiencing new meanings and knowledge.

Another aspect of our philosophy of education is working together with other teachers, parents, and the *atelierista*—a teacher with knowledge of art and art materials. The atelierista helps students make their thoughts and interpretations real using wire, clay, paint, and other art materials in the atelier, or art studio. The children's representations become artifacts of their learning. Having a studio gives the students time and space to think, practice, and learn techniques for handling materials.

The students' artifacts in different languages are organized by teachers in documentation panels, displayed on the classroom's walls to make learning visible to the students, teachers, and visitors. As students develop knowledge and ideas, more panels and artifacts are exhibited in the class. Showcasing the artifacts also helps keep the students' interest in the study alive. Children and teachers revisit the documentation and challenge the students to use other media they have not yet used to express their ideas. This is the richness of believing and valuing the students' mental and verbal capacities, their minds, their experiences, their new knowledge.

Parents play a crucial and integral role in our Reggio Emilia classroom. We ask parents to collaborate with us in our class studies in different ways. Teachers see them as partners in their children's education.

My Classroom and the Study About Nature

That year my preschool class had twenty four-year-old students, all from a Latino background. Half of the class were girls, and the other half were boys. The majority came from Spanish-speaking families. The class showed a great enthusiasm to learn, experiment, discover, and take on novel ideas through new experiences and challenges. The students' hundred languages and more directed this study. The trees became visible for the children during our morning conversations when they talked about trees and other things they saw when they came to school. We took up this inspiration when students realized they could see a tree through the classroom window. They were curious and interested in knowing more about this tree. This also sparked the teachers' imagination and increased their interest in trees and nature. The class was ready to learn. What I needed to do was to follow their interests and guide them. The study began with what I call "encounters" with the trees, which included visiting the trees in the neighborhood and in the local park.

Visiting the trees to water them

Visiting the Tree

The class (teachers and students) started having encounters with the trees, talking to them, hugging, touching, and becoming more and more familiar with them. Children were curious and eager to learn everything about the trees and how they behaved and how to take care of them. How did the teachers realize the students were ready to study nature from trees? They listened attentively and interpreted what the students expressed through their comments and questions, as well as their conversations, drawings, gestures, actions, and their many other languages.

Javier: "The tree is almost without leaves."/ *"El árbol esta casi sin hojas."*

Susana: "There are trees that do not have leaves."/ *"Hay árboles que no tienen hojas."*

Oskar: "Look! A trunk." / *"¡Mira! Un tronco."*

Rosa: "I am putting some soil for the tree to get bigger. This tree was small, now is growing."/ *"Le estoy colocando tierra al árbol para que crezca. Este árbol era pequeño, y ahora está creciendo."*

Oskar: "Trees do not have apples. Just trunk." / *"Los árboles no tienen manzanas. Solo tronco."*

Dayanara: "Here is the twig of the tree over there . . . and the leaves are green. There are more tree roots." / *"Aquí hay una rama del árbol, allá . . . y las hojas son verdes. Hay más raíces de árbol."*

Maria: "The outside tree has many leaves of different colors." / *"El árbol de afuera tiene muchas hojas de diferentes colores."*

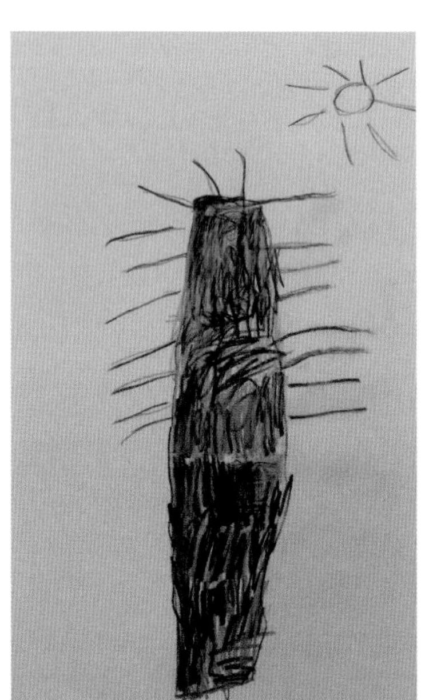

Child's drawing of a tree with branches along the side

Luka: "This is what they have inside. Something for the trees do not fall." / *"Esto es lo que ellos tienen adentro. Algo para que los árboles no se caigan."*

Javier: "Twigs, trunk, and leaves." / *"Ramas, tronco y hojas."*

Susana: "Yes, big tree, leaves, and many twigs." / *"Sí, árbol grande, hojas y muchas ramas."*

After the exploration, the students gathered their ideas. During small groups, they made observational drawings about the experience with the tree. They could also see the tree through the window. One student, Linda, drew the tree with colored markers. While drawing, she made the following comment:

"The tree with branches . . . many. I like it." / *"El árbol con ramas . . . muchas. Me gusta."*

Later we revisited this experience and created new observational drawings of our tree, this time with pencil. We instructed the students to place their pencil drawings under a plexiglass board so they could see their drawings. Then they painted over their drawings using a brush and acrylics on the plexiglass.

Nathan: "I saw snow in here and in the branches." / *"Vi nieve aquí y en las ramas."*

Teachers encouraged the students to write and dictate stories of their art creations made with various media, such as drawings, paintings, clay, wire, and rocks. These stories helped teachers get a big-picture understanding of the students' overall development and learning in other areas, such as oral and written language. The documentation was exhibited on the classroom walls for students and teachers to revisit, discuss, and make comments.

But the students wanted to go further, and they wanted to see and visit other trees, to compare them and come up with some additional conclusions.

From the Class to the Neighborhood to the Park

We began taking walking trips to study other trees around the school. Children made comments about what they saw, touched, and encountered with the trees. The teacher's role was to provoke conversations as well as to reflect with the students about their experiences with nature. Now knowledge became more visible and richer for them. It was time to extend our visits over to our neighborhood park, Riis Park, located about three blocks from our school.

Students, teachers, and volunteer parents all took along clipboards, paper, and pencils. The students made observational drawings about their encounters. The adults took notes about the students' comments, conversations, and questions. The children always surprised us with their ideas, hypotheses, and comments. They were motivated and involved. The teachers were very attentive in taking notes on the students' words and thoughts. Teachers showed great respect and interest surrounding the student's suggestions and experiences. Children flourish when they know they are listened to and valued for what they know, what they say, and what they discover.

Back in class, students explained their observational drawings. This activity allowed the students to expand their ideas of what they observed and learned. Teachers also read aloud fiction and nonfiction stories that reinforced the study and provided opportunities for children to make connections and construct new meanings of knowledge.

Children always look for real experiences that allow them to discover and learn while expanding their curiosity through engaging with real natural objects. Therefore, visiting the park, observing and being part of nature, experiencing the world through the senses by touching, looking, smelling, feeling, and listening is the real-life learning children need to literally *make sense* of their world. From this experience, children will grow their capacity to create, wonder, reflect, and discuss their opinions. They may present their theories and become critical about the natural events they discover, just as they did with our trees.

Urban green spaces come in various forms. From small lots of less than a quarter of an acre to large parks of sixty acres or more, each allows urban children to engage with nature in their community. As discussed elsewhere in the book, Sobel and Ernst (2023) provide intriguing findings showing that children's executive function and resilience develop better when exposed to "some nature" (29) than no nature at all, and full-time exposure to nature does not appear to develop these attributes any more than just some nature. This means that even small natural spaces provide children with the ideal environment to develop their executive function and resilience. Many, if not all, schools, child care programs, and other early childhood settings can identify small green spaces either on their properties or in their communities to provide city kids with the green spaces they need to grow and develop. These green spaces can be an extension of classroom learning, providing opportunities for science, literacy, math, and language development inherently.

The Trees at Riis Park

It was time for the students to expand their interest in trees by walking to Riis Park. Each visit had a specific purpose that we discussed in class before the trip. The students walked to the park with this objective in their minds. During the first encounter with trees at Riis Park, students were curious about what they were going to find and how the trees were doing. They questioned each other: Did the trees have leaves? Are they alive? They compared the trees. They saw how they were changing through the seasons and started getting a close connection with the trees. I could say that the students were establishing a kind of relationship with the trees.

During the class conversation following the visit to Riis Park, I asked the students: "What did you like about the trees you saw at the park? Why?"

> "I liked the trunk because it was soft." / *"Me gustó el tronco porque era suave."*
>
> "I like the whole tree because it has leaves down on the ground." / *"Me gustó todo el árbol porque tenía hojas, hasta en el suelo."*
>
> "The tree branches, because it did not have leaves." / *"Las ramas del árbol, porque no tenía hojas."*
>
> "The tree fell down, and also the squirrel." / *"El árbol se cayó y también la ardilla."*

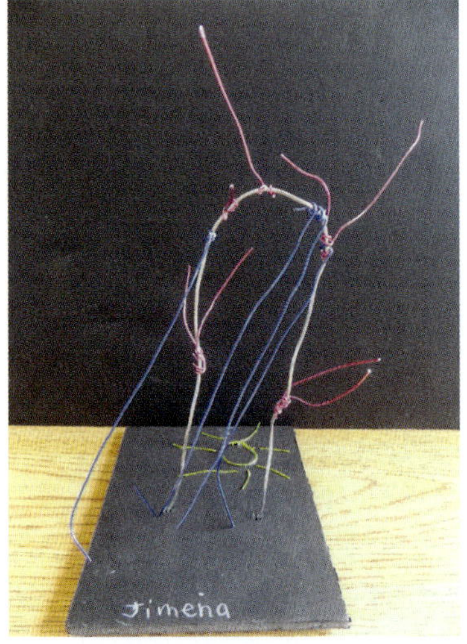

Child's representation of their tree using wire

Students were beginning to see nature with sensitive eyes and even with their feelings. They started to relate to a tree, to understand through their own experience of touching and feeling what a tree and what nature meant for them. Through the activity, students seemed to be developing a connection with nature, a relationship with the trees that they felt comfortable expressing to themselves and their peers. This developing connection reminds me of a beautiful metaphor from Luigi Bellini, a teacher of infants and toddlers in Reggio Emilia, Italy. He wrote, "The trees seem to call to the children, attracting them by their presence, evoking narrations" (Cavallini et al. 2008, 20).

The Fascination with Leaves

Each time we returned to the park, the children examined the trees in more detail. They were fascinated when the leaves changed colors and fell from the trees. During their visits, students collected different types of leaves, and in the classroom they classified them by colors, sizes, and shapes, embarking naturally on this math activity. Students did observational drawings, first using black permanent marker and then painting their drawings with watercolors, trying to reproduce the leaf colors.

We easily integrated mathematics and language arts, both written and oral language, into these visits and observations, as well as science concepts involving the study of nature. While the children painted leaves one day, teachers captured this conversation, in which the children shared theories about why leaves change colors:

Luis: "Why do leaves have other colors?"/ *"¿Por qué las hojas tienen otros colores?"*

Maria: "Because this one is brown and this one is yellow." / *"Porque esta es café y esta es amarilla."*

Margarita: "Because with the rain they fall and change." / *"Porque con la lluvia ellas se caen y cambian."*

Javier: "They are always green. In another week, they may be of another color." / *"Ellas (hojas) son siempre verdes. En otra semana, pueden ser de otro color."*

Luka: "Then, if they get dry, they get dry of other colors."/ *"Entonces, si se secan, se secan de otros colores."*

Leon: "When the fall comes, leaves change colors." / *"Cuando el otoño llega, las hojas cambian de color."*

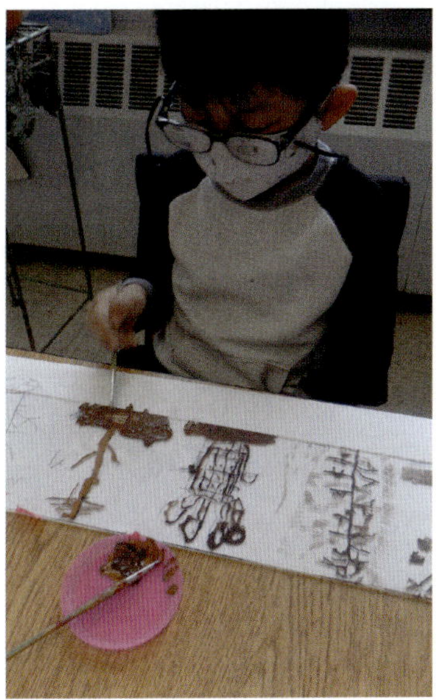

Child using paint to represent the trees

Adopting a Tree

After visiting the park one more time, the teacher guided a conversation with the question: "What did you wonder about during this visit to the park?"

Child writing what he thinks Max, the tree, feels. The child wrote, "*Se siente feliz. Max, ramas.*" (It [the tree] feels happy. Max, branches).

Luka: "I saw many trees in the park." / "*Vi muchos árboles en el parque.*"

Alex: "I liked one big tree with leaves. I picked this *(showing a twig)*." / "*Me gusto un árbol grande con hojas. Agarré esta (mostrando una rama).*"

Margarita: "I love all the trees. And they love me. I want to hug a tree." / "*Me gustan todos los árboles. Y ellos me quieren. Quiero abrazar un árbol.*"

Linda: "I liked the trees very much." / "*Me gustaron mucho los árboles.*"

Leon: "Big trees and small trees." / "*Árboles grandes y árboles chicos.*"

Luka: "I want a tree." / "*Quiero un árbol.*"

Linda: "I bring water for the tree." / "*Yo traigo agua para el árbol.*"

Teacher: "I have an idea. Let's go back to the park to pick a tree to adopt." / "*Tengo una idea. Volvamos al parque y escojamos un árbol para adoptarlo.*"

Javier: "What is *to adopt*?" / "*¿Qué es adoptar?*"

Teacher: "Does somebody know what it is to adopt?" / "*¿Alguien sabe que es adoptar?*"

Leon: "When dad takes a child and gives food." / "*Cuando papi toma un niño y da comida.*"

Margarita: "Lives at home." / "*Vive en la casa.*"

Javier: "Like another son at home."/ "*Como otro hijo en casa.*"

Teacher: "Great answers. Do you want to have a tree from the park to help him like another son at the house?" / "*Maravillosas respuestas. ¿Quieren tener un árbol del parque para ayudarlo como otro hijo en casa?*"

Whole Class: "Yes!" / "*¡Sí!*"

The following visit was very meaningful. Students walked to Riis Park looking for a tree to adopt. The choice was easy for them, and they adopted a tall tree full of leaves of different colors. It was important to our classroom community to find a name for our tree. In class they proposed four names—Spiderman, Rainbow, Max, and Unicorn—and voted. Max was the winner. Spiderman had four votes, Rainbow had two votes, Unicorn had three votes, and Max had five.

Now Max was part of our class. The children wanted to visit Max to see how "he" was doing. The next visits to Riis Park to see Max had specific goals, led by the students: giving him water, cleaning the space by picking up leaves and garbage, observing his branches and his trunk. They also took care of Max by giving him hugs and talking to him, expressing their love. They wrote messages that they hung on the tree's branches.

Working with the Atelierista

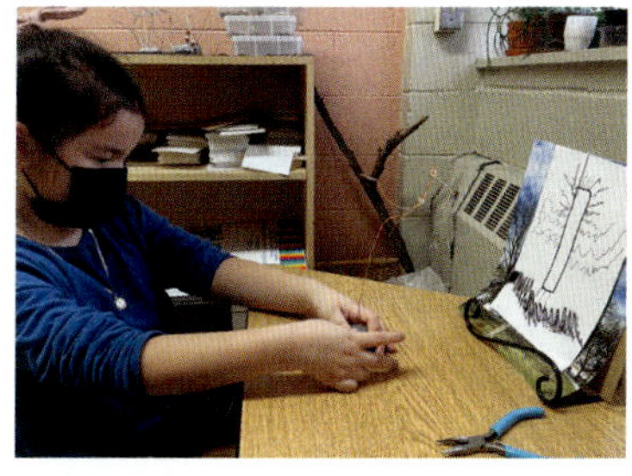

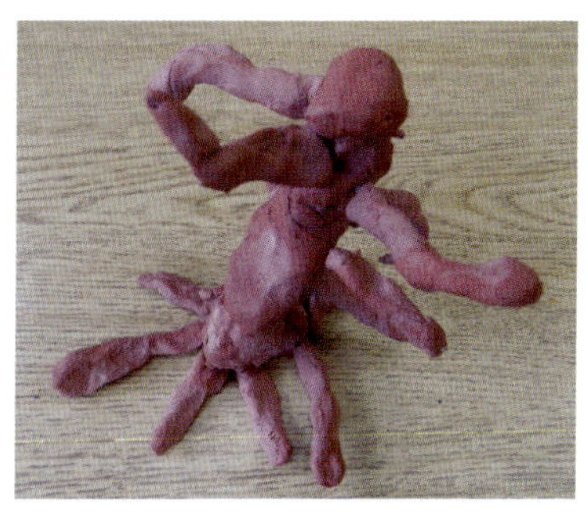

Throughout our study, we collaborated with the *atelierista,* Mr. B, and other classrooms in our preschool building. One day in the spring, Mr. B accompanied the class to affix the students' most recently written messages to Max's branches and encountered another preschool classroom from our building also exploring the park. We introduced this other classroom to Max and soon planned a visit to their room for our students to explain their study, inviting the other students to give Max a hug, to create their own Max drawings, and to write him messages.

Throughout the year, the students engaged in material explorations of wire and clay in the studio with Mr. B. One example of how the studio supported the evolution of the study happened after students developed fluency with the language of wire. They were challenged to cut pieces of wire and (with teacher support) glue them onto transparency paper to cover photos of the tree, creating 2D representations of Max with wire.

Later, students used their black marker drawings of the tree as references to create 3D wire representations of the tree. Children did the same with clay back in the classroom. This ongoing collaboration between the classroom, the studio, and the atelierista is a key aspect of keeping a long-term study like this alive and moving forward.

In the Reggio approach to early childhood education, the use of materials plays a foundational role in the construction of learning. Children develop theories and curiosities about topics and use different materials to explore their understanding. For example, a group of children wondering about the lives of worms may use clay to build the types of homes they imagine worms to live in. Materials are open-ended and intentionally introduced by educators. These can include anything from traditional art media such as paint, clay, and markers to natural materials such as leaves, branches, and stones. Materials are intentionally introduced over time so children learn the properties of each, coming to use these materials as another "language" to express their curiosities and understandings. Over time the materials become a physical manifestation of the children's cognitive development about their topics of study. For example, early understandings of the worms may show simple shapes familiar to children, then as children learn more and research, the worm homes may come to include specific items worms use, the other animals that may be present, the activities worms may do in their homes, and the food worms may eat. For more information about Reggio Emilia, visit the Additional Resources at the end of the book.

Students and parents represent Max using clay

Students using acrylics to make a mural representing the park and Max

Culmination of the Study

At the end of the study, the class participated in a parent-child activity using wire and clay, the same materials the students had been using all year. The children were familiar with the materials in their classroom work, which helped them in developing their theories about Max, while the parents were familiar with the study from the children's conversations and from little projects students did at home. The two groups were able to work together to create various representations, collaboratively building a shared image of Max. One group of parents and students used clay, and the other group used wire. The teacher put together all the artifacts the group made, including the trees made of wire and clay and the photographs that inspired them, to create an exhibition in the class for the students and occasional visitors.

To end the year, students across the entire preschool program used clay and natural materials they collected from the park to create "nests" that they delivered as gifts for Max. Students from every classroom delivered their nests to Max, encircling the tree and singing nature songs they had learned throughout the year. The way Max strengthened community within our classroom as well as across our wider preschool program became clear in this culminating activity. Our hope is that students also saw how Max belongs to a wider community within the park. In fact, many community members who gather in Riis Park continue to share with teachers their memories of seeing our students visit this tree during the "year of Max."

Students finished the academic year with the feeling of taking care of nature. They learned to keep alive the idea that they are surrounded by a community of trees to love and care for so they can grow and provide people with food and air.

All of the children's representations of Max using multiple materials

Reflection Questions

1. As an educator, what impact do you think a study of nature will have on the students' lives in the short term? In the long term?
2. How might parents see nature and parks after they have been part of a nature study with their children? In what ways might a long-term study with nature enrich the parent-child relationship?
3. As an educator, might a long-term nature study transform your own perspective about nature? In what ways?
4. Think about the natural elements you encounter in a natural area near you, such as a park in your community. How can you foster a deeper connection to this natural area by bringing small elements of it into the classroom? How could you create a similar connection with a natural element by visiting the park?

References

Cavallini, I., T. Filippini, L. Trancossi, and V. Vecchi, eds. 2008. *The Park Is…* Translated by J. McCall and L. Morrow. Reggio Children.

Sobel, David, and Julie Ernst. 2023. "Some Nature Is Better Than No Nature: Bridging Research and Practice." Exchange Press, 271. https://hub.exchangepress.com/articles-on-demand/19958.

Additional Resources

Reggio-Emilia Approach

Antioch University New England
www.antioch.edu/academics/education/certificates/reggio-emilia-approach-cert-aune/

Boston Area Reggio Inspired Network (BARIN)
https://bostonreggionetwork.org

California International Reggio Center
www.lascuolasf.org/learning/

Project Zero: Harvard Graduate School of Education
https://pz.harvard.edu/professional-development

Reggio Children
www.reggiochildren.it/en/rc/education/

School Gardens/Food

Farm to Early Care and Education
www.farmtoschool.org/our-work/early-care-and-education

Story Dictation

Boston Public Schools: Department of Early Childhood
www.bpsearlylearning.org/storytelling/dictation

Illinois Early Learning Project
https://illinoisearlylearning.org/tipsheets/young-dictate/

National Association for the Education of Young Children (NAEYC)
www.naeyc.org/resources/pubs/tyc/feb2015/listening-childrens-stories

Index